This book is
personally dedicated to

Gene White

by

a special edition from

GREAT NORTHERN

EDGE *of* HEAVEN

THE YORKSHIRE COAST
PERSONAL REFLECTIONS FROM OUR FINEST WRITERS

Edited by

LEE HANSON

Featuring contributions from:
Ian Clayton | Margaret Drabble | R.J. Ellory | Lee Hanson
Roy Hattersley | David Joy | Ian McMillan | W.R. Mitchell
Blake Morrison | Alan Plater | Martin Wainwright

Introduced by

SELINA SCOTT

GREAT-N-ORTHERN

Great Northern Books
PO Box 213, Ilkley, LS29 9WS
www.greatnorthernbooks.co.uk

ISBN: 978 1 905080 878

Design and layout: David Burrill

CIP Data
A catalogue for this book is available from
the British Library

Supported by

YORKSHIRE POST

Welcome
to Yorkshire
yorkshire.com

'When we go back to the sea, whether it is to sail or to watch - we are going back from whence we came.'
John F. Kennedy.

The Yorkshire Coast at Flamborough. (Rod Slater)

A lone surfer heads towards the sea and spray on Scarborough Beach. (Yorkshire Post Newspapers)

About This Book

There have been numerous books published about the Yorkshire Coast: books about its people, important historical events, famous individuals, its geology and geography, its native fauna and wildlife, its industries and occupations, its towns, its villages and its principal landmarks. This book is none of them and in some small way it is all of them. It contains history but is not historical; it is topographical but is not topography; it is illustrated but is not solely a pictorial record; it records travel but is not a travelogue or tourist guide; it makes reference to wildlife but is not natural history; it describes life and work, people and places, but is not social history or commentary or biography. It touches on the lives of some great authors, but is not a literary guide to the area.

The *Edge of Heaven* is a collection of personal responses from a group of exceptional writers. None were given a brief, nor were they commanded to write in a particular style or to an agreed format. The context was straightforward: tell me what you would like to write about and then write it - in whatever way you wish. The varied responses, styles and topics that have emerged are what make this book unique and distinctive.

You are invited on an unusual and unique excursion around a familiar part of Yorkshire, to see the county's coastline as though it is new, as if seen for the first time. That is what each contributor has managed to achieve.

Lee Hanson, Yorkshire 2011

ACKNOWLEDGMENTS

I am indebted to all the contributors: Alan Plater, Dame Margaret Drabble, Ian Clayton, Selina Scott, Blake Morrison, Roy Hattersley, R.J. Ellory, Martin Wainwright, David Joy, Ian McMillan and Bill Mitchell. Their creativity and skill is the backbone and essence of this book. Particular thanks to Shirley Rubinstein for her strength and kindness in making Alan Plater's contribution available for inclusion. It was with great sadness that we at Great Northern learned of Alan's passing. It turns out that his contribution to this book was the last thing he wrote. I am immensely proud that his final words are within the pages of this book. His spirit lives on.

Thanks to Barry Cox and David Joy at Great Northern Books for liking the idea and allowing me to run with it. Thanks to Liz Slack and Patricia Lennon and everyone else at Great Northern Books headquarters and to David Burrill for the excellent design and layout and also for help with the title. I am most grateful to Rod Slater for a wonderful set of photographic images and for finding the time and energy to visit the coast on demand. Gratitude also goes to Janice Hardman for her technological wizardry. For other photographs I am thankful to David Joy, Bill Mitchell and Yorkshire Post Newspapers.

The paintings on pages 80, 188 and 189 are courtesy Tennants Auctioneers.

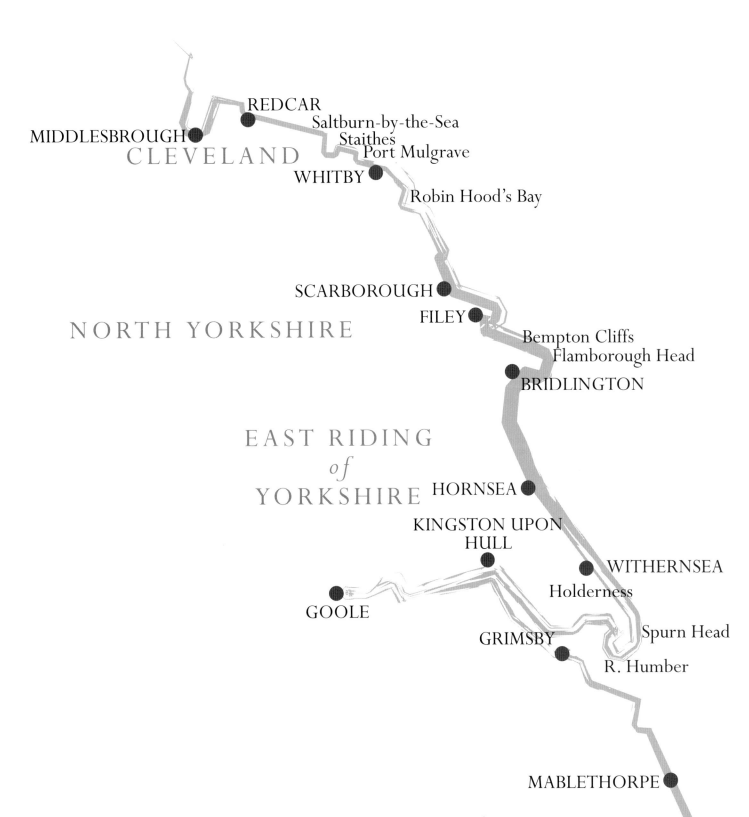

REDCAR

MIDDLESBROUGH

Saltburn-by-the-Sea

Staithes

CLEVELAND

Port Mulgrave

WHITBY

Robin Hood's Bay

SCARBOROUGH

NORTH YORKSHIRE

FILEY

Bempton Cliffs

Flamborough Head

BRIDLINGTON

EAST RIDING
of
YORKSHIRE

HORNSEA

KINGSTON UPON
HULL

WITHERNSEA

Holderness

GOOLE

Spurn Head

GRIMSBY

R. Humber

MABLETHORPE

LINCOLNSHIRE

SKEGNESS

The clean sea, the rich rock pools, the quiet of South Landing, Flamborough. (Yorkshire Post Newspapers)

Foreword

SELINA SCOTT

"The strange alchemy of 'place', forged in the main by Yorkshire folk who've gone before with those who live there now is explored in this book on a poetic scale."

It always gives me a funny feeling, thinking about the Seaside. As a child growing up in 1950's Yorkshire, we never talked about The Coast, we dreamt of far more exotic destinations: Scarborough, Whitby, Bridlington, Filey, Flamborough, like so many fanciful nations, a huge distance apart. Where were we going to go for our holidays? Which would we choose? We took it all for granted: the clean seas, the rich rock pools, us, the only family on the beach on the quiet South Landing at Flamborough. Happy childhood memories come tumbling through. Feelings I never want to have unravel.

Bits of evidence still hang around in boxes in my attic. A snap taken on Scarborough beach, by one of the many roaming press photographers, of a child scowling up through her legs at the camera. Having bypassed the crawling stage, I'm learning to walk, intent on reaching the sea, fast, like a baby crab. A bathing costume, faded, once sunshine yellow and ruched, bought from Rowntree's department store which stretched inch by inch as I grew up on the water's edge. And a sepia ticket kept after I saw my first movie, Bambi, with my father, in Scarborough's dark, warm picture house one summer's afternoon when it bucketed.

What most remains in my memory is the journey to the sea, often in a slow old car, crammed with overexcited children on one of the hottest days of summer. The anticipation, the joy of hearing and then seeing the dead-straight deep blue line of water on the horizon, in the distance, has never left. You know what I mean.

Not all the contributors in this fascinating book are from Yorkshire. What they have to say, however, is timely. Too much misguided modernisation has taken chunks out of this, the most evocative coastline of Britain. Whitby lost its fishing cottages, climbing up its north shore, in the lee of 7th century St Hilda's back in the 1960's. One bad decision on this scale today will wipe out the very essence of what it means to be close-knit. Today, the town is threatened on its green approach with superstore development. Fishing communities built from shared family tragedy still have a handhold but the commercial pressures are immense.

The strange alchemy of 'place', forged in the main by Yorkshire folk who've gone before with those who live there now is explored in this book on a poetic scale. Captain Cook's spiritual resonance in modern day Whitby means much to one writer in this book. Elsewhere Dracula has a walk-on role. No wonder. The lure of the 99 steps to the abbey on the cliff on a darkening winter's evening is still a spook's delight.

All we most treasure about our Coastal heritage, seen through the observation and imagination of some of Britain's finest writers, is laid before you in this fascinating book.

The Yorkshire Coast:
An Introductory Overview

BY LEE HANSON

There was a feeling of freshness and vigour in the very streets, and when I got free of the town, when my foot was on the sands and my face towards the broad, bright bay, no language can describe the effect of the deep, clear azure of the sky and ocean, the bright morning sunshine on the semi-circular barrier of craggy cliffs surmounted by green swelling hills, and on the smooth, wide sands, and the low rocks out at sea – looking with their clothing of weeds and moss, like little grass-grown islands – and above all, on the brilliant, sparkling waves. And then the unspeakable purity and freshness of the air.

Anne Bronte, from Agnes Grey *(1847)*

Anne Brontë's words are proof, if any is needed, that praise for the beauty and splendour of Yorkshire's coastline goes back a long way. Scarborough held Anne in such thrall she not only chose it as a location for both her published novels but also as the place to spend the final days of her life. Scarborough was, quite simply, the place 'where she would be happiest'. Her sister Charlotte recorded that Anne passed away serenely in an armchair, gazing out over South Bay and the castle – the view she loved so much. The doctor who attended her remarked that he had never seen such a 'fixed tranquillity of spirit'. One can only guess what thoughts must have passed through her mind as she slipped away.

A marked grave in St Mary's Churchyard is all that is left of Anne Brontë in Scarborough, yet her words and what she looked out upon remain. Her descriptions no doubt did much to heighten Scarborough's appeal and draw in visitors, for it was around the time of her death (1849) that Yorkshire's coastal settlements became much more than fishing ports and quiet sites of health and restoration. Fast access by rail and an increase in wealth for those toiling in Yorkshire's manufacturing centres meant that resorts such as Scarborough, Whitby, Filey and Bridlington became prime locations for hordes of Victorian families, who for the first time, could afford to holiday by the sea.

Over 160 years later the appeal of the Yorkshire coast is as strong as ever. A 2003 Countryside Agency *Annual Day Visitor Survey* found that five million day trips were made to the seaside in the Yorkshire region annually. They also calculated that these numbers generated around 87 million pounds to local economies. In

'Some of the old narrow streets [of Scarborough] are as captivating as Chester's, and it has been said that the old houses and the red funnel of the ships below the grey castle are not unlike Gibraltar. Nature clothes the cliffs with glory, and there is sheer loveliness in the walled old gardens and the grandeur of the massive ruins of the castle. The hotels are like palaces; the promenades are fit for kings.'
Yorkshire North Riding, Arthur Mee, 1941.

Scarborough - South Bay and the castle reflecting the early morning sunshine. (Rod Slater)

Top: Coastal erosion at Aldbrough. Management of the hungry North Sea remains a vexing issue along the Holderness coast. (Rod Slater)

Bottom: Erosion is not confined to the flat coastline of Holderness. This sign at Filey Brigg presents a clear warning to walkers. (Rod Slater)

Scarborough Borough alone the tourist industry accounted for around 18% of the workforce. It is clear that the nation's appetite for a trip to the seaside is huge and undiminished. And where better to make that trip than Yorkshire?

The sea-coast of Yorkshire is often said to be the finest in England, perhaps only Cornwall and Devon can rival this claim. Yet the Yorkshire coast is a coastline of two halves. North of the Humber estuary from Spurn Head to Bridlington, the Holderness shoreline is flat and flaky, and although underlain by chalk is nearly all glacial boulder clay. At its highest point it only reaches around twenty metres above high water mark and its mudflats and general landscape probably have more in common with the Netherlands than the rest of Yorkshire. It is often thought of as a lonely and deserted area of shore and it is not difficult to imagine Viking longboats approaching on the horizon for in places little has changed since the days of their invasion. Holderness is a moody, tame and lonely shore.

Lonely it is too for the abandoned houses and caravans that can be seen perched on the edge of the crumbling cliffs at Skipsea, Aldbrough and Barmston. Suspended in mid-air above the sands they wait for the hungry sea to claim them, for here the North Sea nibbles away at the coast at around two metres a year – which equates to about two million tonnes of eroded material. All is in flux with much of this broken material building itself back into the coastline further down the shore at Spurn Head. Coastal management is as vexing an issue now as it was 30 years ago. It is an issue for the whole coast, but more so here. In 1991 almost two million pounds was spent on two rock groynes and a rock revetment to protect Mappleton and the B1242 coastal road. Work is ongoing.

The flat expanse of the Holderness countryside pays dividends though. In summer the fertile land is a green and gold sea of corn and barley. Everything is so level that distant farm buildings and trees appear inverted in the sky in strange mirage effects. Great architecture is easy to view and if churches are your thing then the sequestered villages of Hedon, Paull and Patrington provide some of the finest examples in the country. Hedon, once one of the oldest boroughs in England (until 1974) is home to the Parish Church of St Augustine. Commonly known as 'The King of Holderness', it dates from the medieval period with the oldest section going back as far as 1190. 'The Queen of Holderness', St Patrick's Church, can be found a little way up the road at Patrington. Similarly dated it is considered to be one of the most beautiful village churches in England and on a clear day its 62 metre spire can be seen as far as 40 miles away. Although not quite in the same league, St Andrew's Church at Paull is a fine building and like its neighbours is also Grade 1 listed. Paull has the added attractions of a privately owned lighthouse, a short promenade and Fort Paull - a gun battery and visitor centre, first constructed under orders from Henry VIII. From here the whole span of the wide Humber Estuary and the port of Hull can be surveyed with ease.

Seven miles of dockland once extended along the banks of the river Humber making Hull one of the country's largest and most important ports. Wedged in the angle where the River Hull meets the Humber it has been a centre of trade since 1160 and pre-dates Liverpool by several centuries. When transatlantic trade made Liverpool expand so spectacularly, it was a Hull man who stepped in to peg it back. William Wilberforce fought successfully for the abolition of the slave trade – an act that removed a large portion of Liverpool's business. Wilberforce's 17th-century Birthplace is now a museum where the story of his life and many of his personal belongings can be viewed.

Although Hull's docks and fishing industry have declined since the 1970s the port still handles around 13 million tonnes of cargo each year and employs several thousand people, which could rise further if improved rail links are completed. The largest compensation for the decline in fishing has been the growth of the roll-on/roll-off ferry services to mainland Europe. The main ferry terminal is found in King George Dock where over a million passengers and more than 10 million tonnes of traffic are handled each year.

Hull has also exploited the retail and leisure markets in recent years. The old Humber Street Dock in the city centre is now a marina with over 270 berths for yachts and small sailing vessels. Prince's Dock has now become The Prince's Quay Shopping Centre and not too far away is The Deep, a museum and aquarium that ranks among the best in the world.

The largest scheme to promote economical and social growth and mobility in the district has been the building of the Humber Bridge. Plans were drawn up for a bridge back in the 1930s but work didn't start until 1972. When opened by the Queen in 1981 it was the longest single span suspension bridge in the world. It has since slid down the rankings to fifth though it remains a magnificent structure. The best way to appreciate the sheer scale of this construction is to walk across it and once up there the whole estuary is before you. Many locals would take issue as to whether the bridge really has liberated the area and facilitated commercial growth. The level of tolls, some argue, has choked off trade and communications. Yet for all the arguments, the coastline of Yorkshire and the city of Hull would be poorer without it. And, incidentally, a walk or a cycle across is free.

Spurn Head (or Spurn Point as it is also known), is a curious three mile spit of sand and shingle that juts out nearly halfway across the mouth of the Humber. Thanks to eroded material washed down from the Holderness coast, the peninsula is gradually growing towards the Lincolnshire Coast and, without fairly constant dredging, would have closed the river to navigation and isolated Hull. Since 1960 it has been owned by The Yorkshire Wildlife Trust and is a designated nature reserve. Thousands of migrating birds fly past and stop off here and many rare species are regularly spotted. A special observatory has been set up for bird lovers to monitor their feathered friends and accommodation can be arranged. Visitors are also likely to see seals, many butterfly species and on occasion roe-deer. Spurn is also an excellent spot to watch shipping on the Humber.

As mild, flat and powdery as the coast might be up to Bridlington there is nothing of a tame nature beyond it. The other half of the Yorkshire Coast is steep, rugged, tough, uncompromising and magnificent.

The mighty bulk of Flamborough Head is succeeded by the great cliffs of Bempton and Speeton. Riddled with cracks and caves, indentations and arches, they are dotted with precarious nests and the raucous cries of thousands of seabirds. Here is the site of one of the RSPB's most famous bird sanctuaries and several carefully installed viewing points give spectacular close-up views of puffins, gannets, guillemots, razorbills, kittiwakes and fulmars. In all, the nature reserve supports colonies of 200,000 nesting seabirds and in 2009 attracted over sixty thousand visitors, making it one of the most visited wildlife centres in the country.

Further up the coast comes Filey Brigg, a long, shelving mass of limestone rock which runs far out into the sea. This heralds the start of what has become known as Yorkshire's 'Jurassic' or 'Dinosaur Coast', a 35 mile stretch of coastline that has yielded ammonites and plant fossils 120 million years old. Most prized are the dinosaur footprints discovered in the sandstone of Whitby's foreshore. From Ravenscar downwards the

Whitby Abbey (Yorkshire Post Newspapers)

'Nobody, who approaches Whitby Abbey in the true spirit of pilgrimage, can look on that broken church on the cliff-top without being moved. In certain lights, specially at twilight and dawn, it takes on an ethereal beauty that I have not seen elsewhere.

Striding through Yorkshire, Alfred J Brown, 1938.

whole area was once a large estuary where three-toed carnivorous theropods and plant-eating sauropods roamed the mudflats for food. Prehistoric fish-lizards and crocodiles have also been found in the limestone and mudstone of the cliffs. It is a treasure trove for palaeontologists and fossil hunters.

Between Filey Brigg and Scarborough are high cliffs indented with rock strewn bays, some accessible, some not. Scarborough's own limestone promontory and its historic castle form landmarks which are seen far out at sea. It is a town of elegant Georgian and Victorian buildings, spacious parks, sandy beaches and a lively harbour. Scarborough was the first British seaside resort and its popularity can be dated back as far as 1626, when a Mrs Farrow proclaimed the restorative qualities of a small, reddish-coloured stream flowing across south sands. It was claimed that this water would purify the blood, open the lungs and could cure, among other things, asthma, scurvy and leprosy. Visitors were encouraged to bathe in and drink the seawater. Quack medicine it may have been, but it did not stop the gentlefolk of England taking up the offer and throughout the 18th century and a large part of the 19th the sands of Scarborough's twin bays were spotted with naked bathers doing themselves no end of good. Women gradually began to cover themselves up, but men continued bathing in the nude right up to the 1860s. To help these goodly people get out to the sea with ease it was at Scarborough where the bathing machine (a roofed and walled wooden cart) was invented. Its use was essential if one was to conform to the correct and 'proper' sea-bathing etiquette. Bathing is still popular, though these days it is done mainly for fun, not for medicinal purposes, and no one purposely drinks the water anymore, nor do they strip down on the beaches or have themselves rolled into the sea from a wheeled cart.

An enduring feature of Scarborough today is the renowned Stephen Joseph Theatre – the first theatre in the round in the UK. Now based in what was once the Odeon cinema, the theatre's continued existence owes much to the talent and fund raising energies of Sir Alan Ayckbourn. Sir Alan is one of Britain's foremost playwrights and acclaimed directors whose work is performed all over the globe. Although born in London he has been associated with Scarborough and the Stephen Joseph Theatre since 1957 – he was permanent Artistic Director from 1972 until 2009. The majority of his plays are still premiered in the town before they transfer to The West End and the world. Those who seek his monument, go visit Scarborough.

Beyond Scarborough are found what many believe to be the finest parts of the coast scenery. The picturesque old fishing villages of the North Yorkshire coast offer a unique antidote to busy city life. Robin Hood's Bay is a curious and enchanting place, where the houses seem to be piled one on top of another, many appearing ready to tumble into the sea at any moment. Its narrow, cobbled lanes all lead to the sea and harbour and the smell of the sea is everywhere. Leo Walmsley set his *Bramblewick* trilogy of novels here and the first of these, *Three Fevers*, was filmed in 1935 as *Turn of the Tide* – a remarkable film and the first made by J Arthur Rank. Walmsley, like Anne Brontë before him, did much to bring the beauty of the coast to inland audiences. Also like Anne he desired the coast as his final resting place. Although based in Fowey, Cornwall when he died in 1966, his ashes were scattered into the sea at Robin Hood's Bay.

Fishing villages with a similar appeal are Runswick Bay and Staithes. Runswick has a singular history as in 1682 a huge landslip dispatched the original village into the sea. The story goes that a wake was underway when a latecomer noticed the house steps slip from under his feet. The startled mourners fled the house and urged fellow villagers to evacuate their homes. By morning, every single house save one had crashed down into the waves. It was reported that the one that survived was the house of the dead man – though which particular house this was is still open to debate. The new village, built on the south side of Lingrow Beck, was for many years still threatened by the possibility of further landslips. In 1970 a new sea wall was constructed and this so far has provided more than adequate protection. Just what the original Runswick looked like is unclear, but the new village is one of the gems of the Yorkshire Coast.

Whitby is the place where Captain Cook learned to sail and where Bram Stoker derived some of the more intriguing details for his 1897 novel *Dracula*. Stoker was so impressed by the dark, menacing aspects of the harbour, the gothic stone abbey, St Mary's Church and the 199 steps that he chose it as the place where the seductive Count arrives in England and meets and kills Lucy. This is not the only literary association. Mrs Gaskell set her novel *Sylvia's Lovers* here. Her Monkshaven is a thinly disguised Whitby, and in the book we are taken back to the period between the Napoleonic Wars when the town was a great whaling centre. Along with Mrs Gaskell, Charles Dickens, George du Maurier, Wilkie Collins and Alfred Tennyson all visited and enjoyed the atmosphere of the town. It is also thought that Lewis Carroll was inspired to write his famous poem *The Walrus and the Carpenter* by long walks on the beach. The novelist Mary Linskell was born in Whitby in 1840 and although she is no longer widely remembered, her *Haven under the Hill* (1886) was a Victorian best-seller. The earliest named English poet, Cædmon, composed his verse here whilst he was a herdsman at the monastery of Whitby between 657 and 680. His only known surviving work is *Cædmon's Hymn*, a nine-line vernacular praise poem in honour of God. Although it is believed that Cædmon's poetry was exclusively religious, one is tempted to think that he was also inspired by the beauty of his surroundings.

As well as writers, Whitby has proved an inspirational base for hordes of artists who have strained and laboured to record the town's charm. Frank Meadow Sutcliffe is perhaps the most famous. His masterful and iconic photographs present us with a complete and revealing picture of the town in the late Victorian period. He won awards around the world for his work and helped lift photography from a pastime into the realms of art and documentary. The Sutcliffe Gallery on Flowergate holds a vast collection of prints and original plates and is visited by thousands each year.

Popular in his lifetime, and now widely regarded as a Victorian master, Atkinson Grimshaw (1836-1893), created several striking atmospheric paintings of the town. Although working in realistic vein, Grimshaw's paintings have a lyrical and evocative beauty about them. He transcribes with great accuracy the rain and mist, the puddles and smoky fog and the twilight of Victorian England, yet manages to avoid the dirty reality of the urban scenes he captured. To many his work is poetry on canvas.

It wasn't just Whitby that attracted Grimshaw. He lived in Scarborough for several years naming his rented house there 'The Castle by the Sea' after a poem by Longfellow. Throughout his career he was always attracted by the sea, ships and docks. The Coast of Yorkshire inspired much of his best work.

North of Staithes at Boulby, the crumbling cliffs reach their highest point – 200 metres above sea level. A little further along at Huntcliff Nab the coastal scenery falls away abruptly and the land lowers itself towards the sea again. The result is one of the finest stretches of beach on the coast and one of the major surfing locations in the North of England. This relatively modern leisure pursuit has given Saltburn by the Sea some renewed significance as a tourist attraction and in 2010 it held a UK Pro-Surf event that showcased the talents of some of the best surfers in the country.

Founded in the mid-19th century through the vision and finance of wealthy industrialist and Quaker Henry

A View of Whitby Harbour by Moonlight, by John Atkinson Grimshaw, (1836-93). His work transcribes with great accuracy the rain and mist, the puddles and smoky fog and the twilight of Victorian England. Many feel that Grimshaw's art is poetry on canvas. (Bridgeman Art Library)

Hull Docks by Night, by John Atkinson Grimshaw, (1836-93) (Bridgeman Art Library)

Whitby Harbour, circa 1880. This image and others enabled Frank Meadow Sutcliffe to lift photography from a pastime into the realms of art and documentary. Interestingly the fishing vessel pictured here hails from Penzance, a clear indicator that at this time Whitby was still an important port nationally and not just the home to locally manned boats. (Copyright Sutcliffe Gallery www.sutcliffe-gallery.co.uk)

Pease, Saltburn-by-the-Sea was intended to be a 'celestial city', built around what was at the time a small fishing hamlet. The first houses built were constructed of white brick and given the names of jewels in keeping with the founder's vision. Within 20 years the main form of the town was complete including railway line and station, hotels, pier, cliff hoist, public gardens and Wesleyan chapel. Henry Pease died way before his plans were realised in full, yet because of his energy it became a hugely popular seaside resort and place to live. It is still a fitting memorial to his vision and is as popular now as it was then. Its Victorian centre is still relatively well preserved.

The biggest reminder of Saltburn's importance as a Victorian bathing resort is the presence of the only remaining pleasure pier in the North East. Opened in May 1869 over fifty-thousand people paid to stroll upon it in the first six months of its life. It is still a major attraction and in 2009 it won The National Pier Society's *Pier of the Year* award. Directly above the pier is the oldest working water balanced inclined tramway in Britain. This cliff railway is still well patronised and will most likely transport visitors to and from the beach for decades to come. It certainly presents an easy option when transferring your surfboard from the town down to the surf.

To make a living off the coast of Yorkshire is as hard now as it was a century ago. Depleted fish stocks and restrictions on the amount of catch make fishing a precarious trade for individual boat owners. It is hard to compete against the super trawlers and international fleets. Many of the cobles that leave Filey, Bridlington and Whitby now carry eager sea anglers on day fishing trips. Those that still fish commercially are more likely to land their catch at Grimsby or Hull than the smaller ports along the coast. Since the cod wars of the 1960s and 1970s only a small proportion of fish auctioned at Grimsby and Hull is caught by local boats. It is now very much a career of diminishing returns.

It is not all doom and gloom however. Bridlington is now Britain's largest shell fishing port with a multi-million pound export market, supplying crabs and lobsters to restaurants and hotels in France, Spain and Italy. The number of boats operating out of the port has more than doubled in the past few years. As with all industries diversity is a key element to survival. The fisher folk of Yorkshire have always been resilient.

Battling the waves and currents of the North Sea is also not a career for the faint-hearted. Even the most experienced seafarers can get into difficulty if the weather turns around. The RNLI maintains six lifeboats along the treacherous coast between Staithes and Bridlington. They are all kept busy. Whitby Lifeboat Station was established in 1802 and since 1966 has been an inshore lifeboat station. Her crews are among the most decorated in the country and have so far been awarded 36 RNLI medals, 5 of which are gold.

The colour and contrasts of the Yorkshire Coast have attracted visitors for over two centuries. The railways brought the seaside within the reach of the great mass of the population in the 19th century; today mass car ownership has brought easy access to nearly all of it. Without difficulty motorists can now seek out remote sandy coves and headlands as well as the more traditional resorts. More people than ever before visit the coast. Some come as people always have to swim, fish, sail and paddle; to observe the local wildlife and fauna; to walk along the clifftops; or simply to enjoy an ice cream on the promenade. Others come to participate in more modern pursuits such as surfing, scuba-diving, mountain biking, windsurfing and waterskiing. The activities may alter; the lure of the sea does not. A measure of peace and beauty can always be found, even in the busiest resorts, and for many, the swaying sound of the sea, its mystery and its magic are enough.

For whatever we lose (like a you or a me)
it's always ourselves we find in the sea

Edward Estlin Cummings

Between Humberside and Cleveland there is a remarkable choice of attractions and scenes. There are glimmering hulking cliffs, sandy promontories and tranquil beaches; busy urban centres and picture-book villages; vibrant resorts and quiet remote hideaways; flattened glacial tablelands and magnificent walls of wave-gouged chalk. It is a place of history and modern innovation; a place of conservation, stunning wildlife and great natural beauty. The contrasts and the variety are the core of its beauty and it is these contrasts that are celebrated in this book. Like all visitors, each contributor has been to the coast and taken away some memories from their time there. Their experiences are recollected here.

The awesome cliffs at Bempton offer some of the most spectacular coastal scenery in England. They also preside over the fragmentary remains of more than 200 shipwrecks. (W.R. Mitchell)

MARTIN WAINWRIGHT

Yorkshire Coast Memories

Born in Leeds, Martin Wainwright is northern editor of the *Guardian*. As well as producing over 10,000 articles Martin is a champion of the countryside and has edited and written many books. His most recent is *True North: In Praise of England's Better Half*. Published by Guardian Books it is a journey through the beautiful, lively, diverse place that is the North of England.

In the piece that follows Martin takes us on a similar journey recalling his associations, experiences and his enjoyment of many parts of the coast.

My first really vivid glimpse of the Yorkshire coast was through the broken mouth of Slam Gutter, a derelict alum works drain between Ravenscar and Boggle Hole. My brother, sisters and I squeezed into it, encouraged by a glimmer of light at the far end. To our amazed delight, this turned out to be an airy ledge where the narrow passage's stonework crumbled away completely, halfway down the cliff.

We had bucketed and spaded before that on the beaches at Redcar and Sandsend, and collected pebbles at Spurn for an aunt to polish in a curious, rumbling machine which she left on when she wasn't at home, to deter burglars. But the wriggle and perch at Slam Gutter was my introduction to something different from sunny afternoons beside the sea. It began a lifelong relish of the drama, excitement and secrecy behind our county's mighty but unstable seashore.

Part of the attraction was that our parents, let alone the Health and Safety Executive, should absolutely never know where we had been. But like all childhood adventures, our crawl also had an educational side; nothing venture, nothing learn. Around the cracked lips of Slam Gutter there were tiny fossils in the seldom-visited cliff-face. I was soon out about with a hammer, discovering examples of my 100 million–year-old predecessor, the ammonite, those evocative twists of former life turned into stone. Part snail, part French horn, they are deservedly a symbol of the Yorkshire coast. Three of them – complete with imaginative snakes' heads - feature on Whitby's coat of arms.

Ammonites lived some 200 million years ago; but our county's seacliffs tell stories even older than that. First parents and then teachers on school outings explained how the cliffs' abrupt slices into the earth's crust reveal a history book which in most of our comfortable, inland Yorkshire was hidden far underground. "Here is the 11th century, 1066 and all that," said Miss Harvey, our class teacher in the last year of primary school, as she prodded a thin layer of dark soil which seemed ridiculously close to the 1950s' surface of gorse and grass. "What year's that then, Miss?" asked Susie Clough, the boldest of us, pointing to the foot of the cliffs, 300ft below. The number of noughts BC in the answer had us all oohing and aahing and, in the longer term, using our small but imaginative heads to realise the scale of wonders on our Yorkshire doorsteps. The television, a rarity which we watched only occasionally at a neighbour's house, was not the only door to adventure. We didn't have to emigrate to find excitement, to Shangri-La or Timbuktu.

Later, I discovered the human story along the coast, both from the past and in the ways that Yorkshiremen and women continue to earn a living today. Slam Gutter's industry, for example, proved to have an extraordinary story to tell: the way that an entrepreneur from York, Thomas Chaloner, broke the Pope's mediaeval monopoly on alum-making (essential for 1000 products, from dye-fixing to cosmetics and – these days – children's Play-Doh) by smuggling skilled workers out of the Papal States in wine barrels. Then there was the part played in the refining process by urine, brought as ballast in coal ships returning empty from London; one of the few benign examples of the capital's age-old tendency to pee on us supposed inferiors in the regions. The stuff of children's giggles, perhaps, but we took the virtues of urine seriously. Other school visits, to Huddersfield and Halifax, had shown us the textile industry's tradition of 'wuzzing', or whirling wool soaked in pee around in an open basket, using centrifugal force to cleanse and dry it.

Just as curious was the work which I came upon as the *Guardian's* local journalist, in Europe's biggest potash mine at Boulby. This sinks below the exceptionally high, 600ft seacliffs on that stretch of the coast north of Staithes, providing half of Britain's agricultural fertiliser from depths exceeded by only one other European mine, in Finland. Nearly a mile down, scientists funded by the Particle Physics and Astronomy Research Council used a bug-eyed device called the ZEPLIN-III Detector between 2003 and 2007 to search for that elusive quarry, dark matter. They had proved the existence in theory of this strange, mind-stretching phenomenon which may account for nine-tenths of the universe, but stubbornly, the thing itself refused - and still refuses - to appear.

Boulby's dark, secret depths had optimum conditions for quietly watching, in undisturbed side passages away from the potash-mining face. Such inaccessibility – the secrecy which goes with the excitement and drama - is central to the appeal of my Yorkshire Coast. I like places which are very difficult to reach, as with Slam Gutter, or completely impossible: pinnacles which you can only visit through the writings of others more daring or nimble. One of my favourite colleagues on the *Guardian* was the late Harry Griffin, whose *Country Diary* was enthralling because he could climb, as a veteran 'crag rat' from the Coniston Tigers mountaineering club, to places which no other guide to the Lake District could reach. Between Huntcliff's former Roman signalling station above Saltburn and the collapsing coastline south of Hornsea, where 40 towns have been lost to the eroding sea since Norman times, there are plenty of such places. Boulby's mine is one; another is Bempton Cliffs.

It took me nearly 60 years to explore these properly and it still surprises me that many people have heard of them only rather vaguely, and sometimes not at all. Scarborough, Brid and Filey can be heaving, but the ribbon of belvederes run by the Royal Society for the Protection of Birds at Bempton – at the end of a lane where your SatNav suggests you are plunging straight into the North Sea are seldom crowded. You rarely have to queue for long, either, at the Ethical Catering Outdoors caravan where Katy Wheelwright, late of the Bean There café in Bridlington, serves her delicious home-cooked food.

The herby cheesejack and lavender scones are awesome, in the modern teenagery sense. The cliffs themselves are awesome in the more traditional use of the word. The highest on the Yorkshire coast and among the tallest in the whole United Kingdom, they drop sheer to the sea. Seamed with gullies and ending, at their base in scaurs, or reefs jutting out into the surf, they preside over the fragmentary remains of more than 200 shipwrecks.

There's inaccessibility again, in spades. There is no way I would ever want to be involved in a shipwreck below Bempton; but the thought of the wind howling, the sea raging and the flimsy lifeline fired on a rocket from the cliff edge to carry out the breeches buoy, sets the imagination on fire. You'll have shared, I'm sure, that wonderful sensation of having a comfortable ringside seat at dramatic events, which you also get from reading Griffin's mountain escapades, or Frank Worsley on Shackleton's escape from Elephant Island and crossing of South Georgia. It isn't the *schadenfreude* of the Germans, deriving pleasure from others' misfortune. More *excitementfreude*, *Yorkshirecoastfreude*, sharing the heroic deeds and hair's breadth escapes of others at second hand.

Every wreck has its own story, and you can read some of them enjoyably in a pile of old photograph albums which the painter Richard Burton keeps in his studio and gallery at Buckton, the neighbouring village to Bempton. None are more extraordinary than the loss and partial salvage of the First World War Royal Navy submarine G3 which foundered in heavy seas in 1921 while under tow for the shipyards on Tyneside where she was to be broken up for scrap. Instead, she was stripped of her valuable parts by Jack Webster, another entrepreneur in the Chalenor tradition, who organised pulleys down the one, just-about climbable breach in Speeton Cliffs, the stretch next to Bempton, and hauled up the sub's two generators and other valuable components. He did a deal with a local businessman, Fred Parker, who sent a traction engine to the clifftop to lug the generators to his small engineering works at Hunmanby, where he also owned two houses. Until the national grid finally reached the village in 1931, G3's former components made the three buildings famous, as they blazed in splendid isolation with the novelty of electric light.

Webster and his workers were in the tradition of the celebrated 'climmers' who made Bempton famous internationally, when they slithered down ropes to harvest the seabirds' eggs. Harvesting was how they described it, and with reason; the taking of a sustainable number of eggs which left the bird population intact. Discredited nowadays, when speedy road transport and international cash would risk over-exploitation, the practice in their day had the sort of common sense often found in any form of hunting, where it is essential for the hunter that there is sufficient prey. I would like to have met climmers such as George 'Owd Lowny' Londesbrough, whose expertise and status as 'the Methuselah of cliff-climbers' was acknowledged by the naturalist Henry Seebohm when he published his *History of British Birds* in 1885. Or the visiting Lancastrian who shinned down and discovered a strangely-patterned rarity which is still known in the record books as the Bury Butcher's Egg.

The climmers are gone, their practice banned in 1954. They join the ghost procession of the military men who manned the RAF's listening post between Bempton and Buckton whose spooky concrete buildings moulder behind a barbed wire fence – just the surface layer of an abandoned complex which was largely underground. Ginger Lacey VC, the air ace, served here; so, as a national serviceman, did John Gorman of the pop group Scaffold whose Lily the Pink was part of the background to my first year at university, in the tumultuous student revolution days of 1968. I wonder if he had any say in the codename Winkle, used for the main 'passive detection' early warning system deployed at the base. But as we try to accustom ourselves to public spending cuts in the wake of the banking crisis, the story of RAF Bempton has unexpected lessons.

'Every visitor loves Bridlington for its fine promenade and its splendid sands, and for the magnificent bays. There are pleasure boats and gay yachts outside the harbour all the summer through, but on grey winter days the waves throw up curtains of spray against the great sea walls, and the fishermen bring home their harvests at the risk of their lives.'

Yorkshire East Riding, Arthur Mee, 1941.

Two views of the prom looking towards Flamborough and also southwards. (Rod Slater)

Opposite: Another view of Bempton Cliffs.(Rod Slater)

In its heyday, it provided the village with a steady income, quite a few husbands and luxuries such as a cinema. When the base closed in 1972, the little economy's lights went out, as abruptly as those across the wold in Hunmanby when the G3's former generators shut down.

The climmers' former prey, by contrast, thrive as never before: more than 200,000 seabirds nest between May and July; by far the largest, accessible colony in the UK. They look and sound like the inhabitants of a whole city of Hong Kong tower blocks or Brazilian *favela* shanty-towns; ledge after ledge of screeching, squawking, piping fluff, adults, chicks and the equivalent of teenagers swooping around in practice flights. There are puffins with their mad beaks, kittiwakes which sound exactly like their onomatopoeic name, fulmars, shags and my own favourite by a long way, the elegant gannets. Those who know this bird only through the metaphor for greedy people who pounce shamelessly on food wherever they see it, may be surprised by its grace. Slim, finely-coloured with a long yellow bill, and powered by long, slender wings which give it the serenity of a glider but much greater speed, the gannet is the aristocrat of Bempton. Birders' telescopes swivel when one soars past.

The second, and I would say essential, way to see the birds and cliffs is from the venerable Yorkshire Belle, a 70 tonne steam launch built in 1947, and with the elegant lines of the time, which plies from Bridlington and often gets the best of the area's unpredictable microclimates. The last time I was at Bempton, in July 2010, the clifftops were wreathed in an eerie sea fret. Far below, we heard the Belle chugging about and even – so well does sound travel in calm conditions over water – the chatter of excited trippers on her decks. Shortly afterwards, we drove down into Brid and arrived just as the ship's puffin cruise was disembarking. "Fabulous," I was told repeatedly by members of an over-60s outing from Doncaster. "We saw that many puffins. And the gannets..!" The mist had been like a half-raised theatre curtain, they said, allowing them a perfect view while we above were wrapped in grey.

Brid is dear to me, although I often wonder what the sensitive T E Lawrence (of Arabia) made of its upfront cheeriness, when he was stationed here in the 1920s, under his alias of Aircraftsman Shaw. There are those who find the seafront brash and even tatty, but I love shops whose buyers have somehow located a source of strange and wonderful souvenirs; brightly-coloured elves supporting a miniature trawler made of matchsticks, or one of my most treasured possessions until I dropped it on our kitchen floor: a mug sliced vertically down the middle and carrying the message: 'You only asked for half a cup of tea.'

This isn't everyone's taste, or indeed cup of tea, but it is a sad mistake to extend a dislike of downmarket kiss-me-quickery into a theory that the whole place is some sad relic of the past. I have heard Yorkshire people – and not only ones from the deadly rival resorts of Withernsea, Scarborough and Whitby – talk about Brid as though it was still in the state that William the Conqueror's Normans left after their Harrying of the North in the winter of 1069. Previously an Anglo-Saxon centre of prosperity valued at £32 in Edward the Confessor's day (think millions in modern money), it was down to eight shillings-worth of land tilled by one farmer and two serfs when the Domesday Book compilers came round in the 1080s.

In reality the little harbour at Brid is bright and bustling, with the sturdy mole giving a solid sense of protection and reassurance that the small craft are safe, so long as they stay in town. Laurence, meanwhile, would at least have liked the powerboat trips round the bay; his job at Brid was to test high-speed inshore rescue craft for the fledgling Royal Air Force. And the presence of handsome Georgian houses should come

The Yorkshire Belle returning to Bridlington circa 1952. This famous boat still offers pleasure trips and private charters between April and October. (David Joy Collection)

as no surprise, from neat terraces in the town to Sewerby Hall, the Grade 1 listed mansion built in 1714-20 and opened as a public museum by Amy Johnson after Bridlington Corporation had the nous and courage to spend ratepayers' money on buying it during the Depression in 1934.

Why no surprise? Because Brid was the birthplace of William Kent, who played a central part in the Georgians' creation of charming, well-proportioned dwellings in beautifully-arranged 'natural' landscapes. Working first with Lord Burlington and then on his own, he earned the lovely tribute from Horace Walpole:

South Bay Bridlington (Yorkshire Post Newspapers)

Bridlington's very own Pirate Ship takes people out on the briny sea. (Yorkshire Post Newspapers)

'Bridlington is two towns in one, the Old Town with the priory and some Georgian streets, and the new town, a seaside resort neither as noisy as Blackpool or Southend nor as self-respecting as Filey.'

The Buildings of England —Yorkshire:York and the East Riding, Nikolaus Pevsner, 1972.

Bridlington harbour and town. (Yorkshire Post Newspapers)

The sea lashes Bridlington's harbour wall. (Yorkshire Post Newspapers)

The ArtsBank Gallery, Saltburn. (Rod Slater)

In 2010 Saltburn held a UK Pro-Surf event that showcased the talents of some the best surfers in the country. (Yorkshire Post Newspapers)

Saltburn is home to the only remaining pleasure pier in the north east.
In 2009 it won The National Pier Society's *Pier of the Year Award*. (Rod Slater)

'Mahommed imagined an Elysium; Kent created many.' Most of them are internationally famous – places such as Burlington's Chiswick House in London or the gardens at Stowe in Buckinghamshire – but one of my favourites is near Brid. The original Buckton Hall, on the town's outskirts and back towards the cliffs, was designed by Kent for the local squire John Robinson. Robinson loved his young wife dearly and had engraved on his new house's main supporting beam: 'Anne Robinson is the prettiest girl in Yorkshire.'

Inaccessibility yet again. That house and the romantic beam were severely damaged by fire in 1919 and the current, gaunt replacement leaves the story, and the graceful world of William Kent and the Robinsons, largely to the imagination. But the architect's youth, as a talented coachwork and signpainter who was sent to study in Rome by local gentry who recognised his talent, has modern echoes. When I was a boy in Leeds, I remember being told that a long-haired, studenty type, who trundled his easel and brushes round the Apperley Bridge valley in a baby's pram, was another talented young artist in the making. His name was David Hockney.

Who, now, is one of the great boosterists for Brid? The same David Hockney, no longer an unknown pram-pusher but one of Britain's most popular contemporary artists. He is a serious figure with clout among the critics, but also a painter with genuinely affectionate everyday followers, perhaps especially because of his use of vivid colours. The Yorkshire coast is often portrayed with a dark palette – the moors and the stormy sea – or with the greys and ochres of a fret. Not by Hockney, who revelled in the brightness of Brid, and the Wolds which lie behind it, when his mother retired there from the family's native Bradford.

In Salt's Mill at Saltaire, his friend the late, great Jonathan Silver hung a series of colour-saturated photos of the resort by the artist, which still line the walls of the 1853 Diner in Sir Titus Salt's former alpaca mill. They blaze out unexpectedly, just as I recall the Union Jack socks of David's brother Paul doing, when I was a reporter on the Bradford Telegraph & Argus and he was a flamboyant Liberal councillor for Idle and later the city's Lord Mayor. Paul was also taken with the light and fun of Bridlington and later followed his mother there, enjoying his own retirement while keeping a helpful eye on David's financial affairs, as a down-to-earth West Riding accountant. The Hockneys' pleasure in the *joie de vivre* of Brid, which matched their own, was completed by the presence there of the brothers' sister Margaret, a nurse who set up a natural medicine clinic in the town.

She is also a talented artist, using a digital camera and flatbed scanner to create striking images, a skill which she learned from attending a Third Age group of older but active Bridlingtonians. Perhaps there's something in the blood. Or is it – and I think that this is more likely – something in the coast? Head north, past the dramatic shoreline of Flamborough, and on via Scarborough, Whitby and the round shoulder of Yorkshire to the mouth of the Tees, and you come to another haven of artists in a delightful town.

Saltburn-by-the-Sea is no Bridlington; there are still genteel long-time residents in the fine villas built by Middlesbrough and Darlington industrialists above the Italian Gardens who might shudder at the comparison. But the elegance which it shares with nearby Marske, where Cliff House recalls the holiday tastes of the Pease family, Quaker ironmasters from Darlington, sits contentedly alongside an artists' colony which is relatively new but really starting to thrive.

One of its supporters is Ian Burke, the 13th Master of Drawing in the 566-year history of Eton College, a grand job title which belies the very local, Teesside nature of the man. Burke's loyalty to his patch – he commutes from an old mill near Danby to Berkshire as a weekly boarder – is now shared by three other members of the school staff who also live on the North York Moors during the holidays and at weekends. Their work, recently collected in an exhibition whose title, Eton Beaks, was drawn from the school's slang for teachers, can often be seen in Saltburn. Down in the town centre, there are excellent galleries such as Andy Hawkins' in Milton Street, where the graduate of the Royal College of Art both paints and sells other artists' work.

Over the road is a newcomer, and a rather extraordinary one. Anyone who collects old toys will know the name of Bryan Goodall, whose Vectis auctions empty the shelves of those who want to get rid of childhood clutter and their opposites, who have display cabinets and dusters ready for every available Matchbox and Dinky toy. A local lad, brought up in Thornaby, Goodall has put £600,000 into renovating Saltburn's former HSBC bank as a meg-art gallery and arts centre; four floors and an attic are packed with wonderful contemporary work from artists who live along the Tees.

The ArtsBank is worth a visit to Saltburn on its own; although the little town's pier, cliff tram (the oldest hauled by waterfilled counterweights in the world) and floral displays will tempt you to turn a day into a weekend and then into a week. It will be excellent if you do, because this part of the Yorkshire coast needs the good, old-fashioned holiday trade to return. The decline of heavy industry, most recently in the closure or mothballing of almost all the Corus steel plants, has devastated the local economy. One of the most alarming stories I pursued this summer for the *Guardian* was a survey in Redcar – my old sandcastle playground – which found that the average visitor-spend in the resort was just £1.70, enough to buy one chip butty or four sticks of rock.

But it is worth going; not just for the good of your soul, which is not always a reliable way of choosing a holiday destination, but entirely on merit. The sands are still fine and vast; if you haven't been to Redcar lately, you may have seen them in the film of Ian McEwan's novel *Atonement* which borrowed Redcar, and many of its residents, to stand in for Dunkirk and the wartime rescue of the British Expeditionary Force by the Little Ships. The donkeys stroll contentedly along, the seafront has a Bridlingtonian zest and the local council is planning a £40 million spruce-up to make it zestier. Local people have also fought a vigorous and successful campaign to preserve the public open space of Coatham Common, which forms a natural seaside foil to the prom's fun and games. And then, paradoxically for coast-lovers, there is the wonderful interior of this part of Yorkshire, the hinterland of the Cleveland escarpment, crowned by the fierce little crest of Roseberry Topping, the Yorkshire Matterhorn.

It is a long time since waves lapped this proud landmark, but the short, sharp trip to its summit includes my ultimate, above-all-else, favourite place connected to the Yorkshire coast. As you tramp steeply up from the National Trust car park at Newton-under-Roseberry, first the Tees appears gleaming behind you, beyond the smokestacks of the former ICI works and other industrial plants. Then, where the path curves left before a second, and final acute clamber to the stone slabs on the peak, the North Sea comes into view across to the East. Here is the perfect eyrie to sit and think about it all; and to travel in your mind down the whole, majestic sweep where our county meets the sea, as far as the lonely lighthouse at Spurn and the reclaimed land – washed round into the Humber from those vanished 40 towns – of Sunk Island.

Brigg End. The Brigg is a unique geological phenomenon, a promontory of rocks and boulders that stretches out to sea. (Rod Slater)

IAN CLAYTON

Time and Place:
My Explorations on the East Coast

Ian Clayton was born and brought up in Featherstone. He worked at various jobs before turning his hand to writing, broadcasting and teaching. He presented YTV's *My Yorkshire* for five series and has published a total of 45 books. His *Bringing it All Back Home* was described by *Record Collector Magazine* as 'One of the best books about popular music ever written'. His latest work, *Our Billie* is an astonishing and heartbreaking account of the events surrounding the death of his nine year old daughter. For more information visit www.ianclayton.info

Among other things he here recounts his love of the Yorkshire coast, his time there recording a television series, *Clayton's Coast*, and also his decision to become a writer. Most interestingly, we learn that the Greenwich Meridian cuts right through the Sand Le Mere Caravan Park near Tunstall...

"There's a time and place for everything." My Granny used to say that a lot, I was never sure what she meant, to be fair I wasn't sure whether she knew what she meant either. It was just one of the many sayings she'd bring out of storage, dust off and throw at me from time to time. Like, "He who laughs last, laughs longest", or "He's as thin as a yard of pump water". Actually she knew very well what that last one meant, because she had pumped many a yard of pump water as a girl whilst looking after her Auntie's geese on a farm up near Sutton-upon-Derwent.

Anyroad, there came a time and a place for me to want to be a writer. I wanted to combine my knowledge of history, both book learnt and personal, with what I knew about geography, both from places I'd seen with those I'd read about, and spice it up with a very rudimentary grasp of science, that I'd overheard in class at Hull Grammar. I spent a lot of the lesson looking through the lab window. The time was the middle of the 1980s, just after the miners' strike, the place was a deep trench that I'd helped to dig into the cliff top near Bempton. My mate, Burt Stevens, and me had been sent to prepare the ground of a new coastguard house for Bridlington. We lodged in an out of season guest house on Marshall Avenue in that town. The weary landlord, this was November, after a busy season, would get us up every morning at 7.00 with a hoarse shout upstairs, "Your breakfast's ready if you want some!". It wasn't the best breakfast I'd had by a long chalk, usually baked beans, a lonesome sausage and a fried egg with black bits on. Burt and me often joked that we ought to buy the landlord a new frying pan from the Woolworths at the top of the street. We spent our day wrapped in three jumpers, long johns and donkey jackets against a wind that whipped across the

North Sea and froze our hands till they stuck to the Hepworth ceramic pipes that we were attempting to lay in trenches. These pipes would then carry away the sewage once the coastguard house was built. We dug a lot of holes and trenches on that job. We spent our evenings drinking pints of Tetley bitter in the Kings Arms. Every night as we weaved our way back to Marshall Avenue, we promised each other that we would walk on the beach next morning and wash our faces in the sea. Yeah! Right! Next morning it was always about to snow or sleet and even at 7 o'clock after a night on the ale, the landlord's lonesome sausage always seemed more tempting than a brisk walk over the shingle.

Now, I mustn't get too far in front of myself here, I want to tell something about my love for the east coast and more particularly I want to write about some invisible geography that's to be found there. I want to tell about a line that's on the map, in fact all the maps of the world, but it's a line that you can't see when you get there. Here goes.

On July 2nd 1881, the twentieth President of the United States, Mr James Garfield, was seeing his wife off at a railway station. After he'd done this and put the hankie that he'd waved with back into his pocket, he stopped to have his shoes shined. Unbeknown to him, an assassin was lying in wait. This assassin was Charles Julius Guiteau, a bit of a loner, who had once been a lawyer after passing a dodgy degree. Guiteau, not a well-liked man, had tried to be part of a religious cult that arranged group marriage. Even in a cult, that was difficult to escape from, he gained the nickname 'Charles Git-Out'. Then one day, or so he said at his trial, he heard a voice from God telling him to shoot the President. Guiteau stalked his prey around the railway station, waiting to strike, he waited until the President waved his wife off, claiming later that he didn't want to upset her and then as Garfield sat down to admire his newly polished shoes, Guiteau fired two shots into his back. He shouted "I am the stalwart of stalwarts and Arthur is President now". He was arrested immediately, brought to trial and within weeks he was hung. His victim lived long enough to see this, for Garfield died a lingering death. Hands that hadn't been washed properly and dirty instruments probed and operated on his back, with a result that infection set in and he too was dead before Christmas. Guiteau's words however had been prophetic, because on the death of the 20th President, the 21st one was sworn in and he was called Arthur, Mr Chester Arthur.

Eighty odd years after this, my Dad, Sid Clayton, found himself working at a packaging company in Featherstone. It was about his fifteenth job in the ten years or so that my Mam had known him. First he worked as a waltzer spinner on the fairgrounds. "The louder you scream girls the faster we go", my Mam screamed the loudest. Then he mixed cake ingredients at Lyon's factory and for a while drove an overhead crane. When my Mam started holding hands with him he was shouting bingo numbers in an amusement arcade at Brid and she was a chambermaid, making the beds and hoovering at the back of dressing tables in a boarding house there. One day at the packaging factory a big roll of brown paper blew over in a wind in the stockyard outside the factory and fell onto my Dad. It crushed his vertebrae and fractured his pelvis. I remember coming home from George Street Junior Mixed as they were lifting him out of the ambulance to stretcher him through our front door. The doctors said that his back injury would mend if he were to sleep on a flat wooden board for a few months. We unscrewed the door that closed off our back kitchen from the living room and he slept on that, watching his favourite programme *The High Chaparral* from a vantage point over near the china cabinet.

My Dad liked 'cowboy pictures', Les Kellett the Saturday afternoon wrestler and songs by The Ink Spots and The Platters. He was a breeder of rabbits and canaries, but he didn't know about much else really. He certainly wouldn't have heard of Hipparchus, the Greek astronomer, geographer, mathematician and father of trigonometry, who nearly two thousand years before the roll of wrapping paper hit my Dad, was working out his ideas on longitude. Or his follower, Ptolemy, who in his book *Geography* imagined the Canary Islands as the start of the world. Or his follower, Marinus of Tyre, a Greek map-maker who plotted the four corners of the then known earth: Ultima Thule, what we know now as The Shetlands, being the north, The Blessed Isles, now the Canaries the west, China the east and The Tropic of Capricorn the south. Marinus of Tyre was also the first man to assign ideas of latitude and longitude to places on his maps.

Now, I can almost hear you saying, "What on earth has all this got to do with the east coast of Yorkshire?". Well here goes. President Chester Arthur, the 21st President of the United States, turned out to be a pretty uninspiring President, but he had one very bright idea, even Mark Twain, the great baiter of office and pomposity conceded that it was a bright idea. And that idea was to call a conference of all the world's developed nations with the purpose of fixing a prime meridian and universal day, so that time and place could be fixed. People in Australia would know what time to get up for breakfast, ships' captains travelling to New York would know what time they would be docking at Ellis Island and passengers on the train departing from Platform One to Hull Paragon at 8.48 am would know when it was 8.48 am. This meridian, to be known as O° Oh Om would scribe a line from the North Pole to the South Pole and would be recognised by all peoples and countries to the west of it and to the east. Up to that point there were many meridians of longitude claiming to be the prime one, Norway had one, Russia did and of course France had their own based on the tip of the Eiffel Tower. Egypt had one based on the Great Pyramid. After much argument and toing and froing, conference decided to adopt a meridian passing through the centre of the transit instrument at the observatory at Greenwich as the initial or prime meridian of longitude. Some had argued for Hipparchus and the meridian that passed through Rhodes, some had quoted Marinus of Tyre and his Canary Islands meridian. San Domingo wanted their own, I can't imagine why, unless they argued that because this was the place where Christopher Columbus first kicked off his shoes to wade ashore in the new world, they had a valid case. And France abstained, typical French! The meridian was accepted that day in October 1884, the same month as my school, George Street Junior Mixed, was being endowed in Featherstone. The meridian would henceforward be known as the Greenwich Meridian and the time on that line would be 'Greenwich Mean Time'. After years of discussion leading up to this momentous moment, conference hoped that if the whole world adopted Greenwich Mean Time, Britain in turn might adopt the metric system, which of course we didn't and still haven't. Typical British!

This Greenwich Meridian starts at the North Pole, passes through the Arctic Ocean, the Greenland and Norwegian seas, the North Sea, the east of England, France, Spain, Algeria, Mali, Burkino Faso, Togo, Ghana, the Atlantic and Southern Oceans, Queen Maud's Land in Antarctica and then joins up with the South Pole.

Now think on this then, if you had a magic surfboard that allowed you to surf the Greenwich line of longitude down from the North Pole, over the Arctic, into the North Sea, clip the tip of Filey Brig and Flamborough Head, the first time you would have to jump off your board to walk on dry land would be on the Holderness coast near Withernsea. To be precise, just outside the village of Tunstall. Even more precisely near to the Sand Le Mere caravan site.

My Dad got round about a thousand pounds compensation for his injuries at the packaging factory. He

Flamborough Lighthouse at sunset. (Rod Slater)

'Flamborough – All the world has heard of its noble headland running far out to sea. One of the most conspicuous promontories and one of the finest viewpoints of the east coast, its white cliffs, for ever beaten by the waves, have been a landmark since the days of the Romans and the Vikings. Yorkshire has few more striking spectacles.'

Yorkshire East Riding, Arthur Mee, 1941.

Flamborough Headland. (Rod Slater)

Flamborough from the air. (Yorkshire Post Newspapers)

wanted to spend it straight away, money never stayed long in my father's pockets, and the first thing he wanted to buy was a static caravan at the east coast. The second thing he bought was a crumby terrace house near Stepney Lane Baths on Beverley Road, Hull. We would be able to have holidays throughout the summer. He didn't give much thought on how we would get there, he didn't even have a car. Neither did he think what sort of holiday it would be for my mother if she was cooking, cleaning and making the beds for three roustabout lads every day. He just wanted a caravan. So a caravan he got. We looked at two sites, one up near Flamborough called Thornwick Bay, which my mother deemed "too hilly for our Andrew", who was recovering from a murmur in his heart and rheumatic fever, and one "down near Withernsea" which we were advised was "nice and quiet and flat". This was the Sand Le Mere Caravan Park and our caravan, a lovely five-berth with a bay window, was taken there on a low-loader in the spring of 1970. We had our first holiday there in the summer of that year, The Kinks sang about 'Lola' from our transistor radio, The Beatles finally called it a day and my mother told us to be careful when we were playing with some kids from the next door caravan. She'd heard that they were from near Barnsley and she thought they might have nits. When we went to the bunk beds our Mam and Dad went to the club on the site. My Dad came home merry on a couple of pints of Hull Brewery Mild and sang *Yellow River* and a song called *Leap up and down with your knickers in the air* to the night sky. The caravan park owner was an avuncular sort of chap with sandy hair and black framed glasses. I think they called him Ellis. I don't know whether that was his surname or his first name. He was just 'Ellis'. He told my Dad off one morning for singing too loud at night, "This is a quiet and decent camp and I'll thank you not to be vulgar", he said. My Dad, who almost prided himself on being vulgar, trumped loudly just as Ellis finished his sentence and then said, "Manners" and followed it quickly with, "Don't worry old cock I'll pipe down a bit". That night he sang every verse of *Leap up and down with your knickers in the air* in between the club and our caravan in a voice like Mario Lanza. Well, in a voice as loud as Mario Lanza.

I didn't know it then, but every time we went to Sand Le Mere near Tunstall, we almost straddled the Greenwich Meridian. For all I knew, the line might have passed straight through the middle of our caravan. I would have been tremendously excited if I'd known then, that every time I knocked the top off my breakfast boiled egg there might have been a fisherman somewhere out in the North Sea searching for crab pots, doing exactly the same thing. Or one on a boat in Lake Togo in Ghana eating his breakfast just like me, or an explorer plodding through the ice in Queen Maud's Land coming back to his quarters to sit down to bacon, because when it was 8 o'clock in the morning in Sand Le Mere near Withernsea, it was that time in all them other places as well. How exciting then, that this invisible geography can link kids in caravans in East Yorkshire with explorers in Antarctica, perhaps pirates in the Atlantic and traders riding camels through the deserts of Algeria.

It's coming towards the Millennium. I'm working as a presenter for Yorkshire Television, I'm scribing my own wiggly line down the east coast of Yorkshire for a series I'm doing called *Clayton's Coast*. I find myself at Patrington to meet a vicar who sports a tattoo on his forearm, a souvenir of his naval years. He's going to show me around St Patrick's Church.

St Patrick's Church in Patrington, known colloquially as the 'Queen of Holderness' is without doubt the most beautiful church that I have ever visited. Simon Jenkins in his book *England's Thousand Best Churches* regards it as a five star job, the highest accolade. He says that its creator, the master mason, Robert de

'The Queen of Holderness'. (Yorkshire Post Newspapers)

Selwicks Bay, Flamborough Head. (Rod Slater)

Patrington, "Is amongst the immortals of the English art". The vicar of St Patrick's tells me that the church is late English Gothic, designed before the Black Death killed off all the best church designers. I love this place, the stone pours down like silver and the spaces inside seem, to my eyes at least, to be perfectly proportioned. It has wave upon wave of arcades and gargoyles peer down at you as though to say, "What are you doing! Walking through all this beauty?"

We made a nice little film at Patrington and stayed in a bed and breakfast there. In the pub that night we talked about the forthcoming Millennium celebrations. Somebody said that instead of building that awful trashy experience thing in the East End of London, they ought to be building something with the vision and lasting gorgeousness of the church here. Everybody sipped ale and nodded. Then the talk came round to who would actually celebrate the Millennium first. Sam our sound recordist said that he'd heard that the first sunrise of the new Millennium would be somewhere in the islands in the Pacific Ocean. Then somebody else said that really the first people who could claim to see in the year 2000 would be just up the road in Tunstall near Withernsea, because that is the first place where the Greenwich Meridian touches the land. A thought flashed through my mind. There's a bloke like my Dad in a caravan at Sand Le Mere Caravan Park and on New Year's Eve of 1999 he's going to raise a glass of mild and sing *Leap up and down with your knickers in the air*! And he will be the first man in the whole world to celebrate the new Millennium.

The next morning I think we went to look for a stone just outside of Patrington that notes that the Greenwich Meridian passes right by this village. Then we headed north on the A165 to meet a man in Filey.

The great Islamic scholar, Al Masudi, who was born in Baghdad in 896 AD, was one of the first to combine a knowledge of history and geography. He visited Russia, Africa and India meeting people from all walks of life, making maps and plotting journeys. He was a man of immense curiosity, a conversationalist, an observer of people. He said in his book, *Meadows of Gold*, that "He who has never left his hearth cannot be compared to the traveller who has worn out his life on journeys excavating the mines of learning and snatching precious fragments of the past from oblivion". What he ought to have added was something my Granny always said when she came back from the seaside, "It's nice going away, but it's always nice to come home again".

At Filey, the day after our visit to Patrington, we met an amateur archaeologist who had dreamed all his life about finding a precious ancient relic. He wanted to show us something that he had dragged to his garden. This bloke's Mam and Dad kept a tea bar at the end of Filey Brigg and he spent his school holidays helping them serve tea and buns to holiday makers in between rock-hopping like a penguin over the boulders and flotsam washed up as the sea came crashing into that headland. He did this summer after summer. Years later, long after the little tea bar with the drop-down front had been retired, he was out walking at the end of Filey Brigg, dreaming up days of splashing summers long past. He walked by the rocks he had hopped on as a lad and noticed something he'd never seen before. It was a large, flat stone with a pattern on it. The pattern was of Fleur-de-Lys. He dragged the stone back to his garden and through research and investigation, discovered that the stone was in fact a medieval coffin lid, that had once enclosed the body of a French knight. All those times before and he'd never noticed it. He might even have jumped in boyhood pumps or sandals on to it while making his way across sea-washed boulders. He dreamed his dreams of discovery and then on the way back his ancient stone found him.

A similar thing happened when I went to meet Dr Peter Halkon further south near Holme-on-Spalding

Moor. Peter is a lecturer in archaeology who studied at Bridlington School and Durham University. One day in 1982 he was doing some digging in a field near Hasholme, in what was the silted up River Foulness, an inlet from the Humber estuary. He saw an ancient piece of wood sticking up. This ancient piece of wood turned out to be a 3,000 year old part of a boat. Much digging later and a team of archaeologists uncovered a complete boat, beautifully preserved, that had been hollowed out from one huge oak tree, thought to be up to 800 years old when it was felled. This boat would have been rowed by 18 men and 2 pilots and plied trade routes around the Humber. Centuries before even Hipparchus and Marinus of Tyre had their ideas about aiding navigation, nearly three millenniums before Chester Arthur's conference, tribes people from East Yorkshire were sailing around the waters of the east coast. I remember saying to him at the time, "This tree, that was a boat, was once an acorn a thousand years before three wise men went to visit a baby in a stable in Bethlehem".

The boat became famously known as The Hasholme Boat and was first preserved at the National Maritime Museum in, where else, but Greenwich, before being shipped to the Beverley Road Baths at Hull, where for two years the public queued to see it being sprayed with a mixture of wax and water. It's still in Hull, continuously treated with polyethylene glycol, pickled forever in a glass case, like those butterflies trapped in nets by Victorian vicars.

The bizarre thing about this find is the fact that Dr Halkon was digging his trench in a field he'd known all of his life, a field he'd played in as a kid. Sometimes we travel a long way to find what was beneath our feet in the first place.

Back on the cliff tops in 1985, Burt and me are trying to prop up an existing sewage pipe in order to connect a temporary one to it. The wind is lashing across the North Sea, my hands are stuck to the pipe, frozen. A mixture of snow and sleet is falling on us. Burt is behind me with a crow bar trying to push the pipe up the muddy trench. The existing pipe slips and cracks. The contents of the pipe begin to seep out, over my hands, up the sleeves of my donkey jacket. I turn round to Burt, he crouches impassively, crow bar resting on his knees. I say to him, "Burt, I'm bloody sick of this type of work. I'm not sure I want to do it anymore".

Burt scowls at me, snow dripping off the lip of his yellow safety helmet. He growls, "What's tha going to do then?"

"I don't know, but I'm fed up of this game!"

Burt thinks, I can see the cogs turning. "Be a writer then! Tha's allus telling me tha can write. Be a writer!"

Now I can't say that at that minute I threw down my shovel and picked up a pen. But it wasn't that long before I started to send off stories to Radio 4. Not that long before Yorkshire TV asked me to present programmes about God's own county and not long after that I was traipsing up and down a line near the Greenwich Meridian doing a series called Clayton's Coast.

As my old Granny said on a regular basis, "There's a time and a place for everything".

A coble waits for the tide. (W.R. Mitchell)

WR MITCHELL

Fishing Villages
of the North East Coast

Birds of the White Cliffs of Yorkshire

W R Mitchell, MBE, Hon D.Litt, is the author of almost 200 books, including several on the Yorkshire coast and its bird life. He was editor of *The Dalesman* magazine for about three decades. Bill's honorary degree was awarded by the University of Bradford. In 2008, the Outdoor Writers' and Photographers' Guild presented him with their major Golden Eagle award. He was said to be one of the founding fathers of outdoor writing.

In these two pieces Bill Mitchell takes us on two personal tours: firstly he guides us through the fishing villages of Robin Hood's Bay, Staithes and Runswick; and then takes a detailed look at the coast's varied birdlife. As is so typical of his style there is a perfect blend of history and personal experience.

FISHING VILLAGES OF THE NORTH EAST COAST

And all along the indented coast,
Bespattered with the salt-sea foam;
Where'er a knot of houses lay
On headland or in hollow bay –
Sure never many like him did roam.

Wordsworth, in Peter Bell, gives us this stirring introduction to traditional fishing villages on the North East coast of Yorkshire. In 1817, three of them were classified by the historian Young as "the great fisher towns of our coast." He had in mind Staithes, Runswick and Robin Hood's Bay. For centuries, a race of stalwarts harvested the sea from small craft known as cobles which, beached when not in use, were in effect boat and harbour in one.

When I toured the former fishing villages on the North Yorkshire coastline in the late 1970s, I was aware from chatting with the old folk of how the lives of the fisherfolk had changed. Once, they formed distinct little communities, handy to their keel boats and cobles. An old chap remarked on the unsociable hours. Many a time he had been up "half the night". He couldn't put to sea when the coastline was ravaged by storms. He added: "Or your luck's out and you haven't much to show at the end of the week."

In my time, women no longer ranged across the scars, looking for fishing bait. Faced with several types of work, young men were selecting jobs with regular hours, fixed pay and pension schemes. The villages of Yorkshire's north-east coastline had become tourist hot-spots. Forty years ago, inspired by the writings of novelist Leo Walmsley, I was able to chat with cloth-capped, blue-ganseyed fishermen, denizens of villages. Most of the fishing activity took place in towns like Whitby and Scarborough. My romantic inclination led me to seek out those who still went down to the sea in cobles.

I also met artists who had been attracted by the colourful forms of buildings in places like Staithes. Dame Ethel Walker, the most illustrious of the fishing village artists, called Staithes "a wildified place." I did not meet her and gazed sadly at what had been her studio when it had been shaken to bits by wind and a wilful sea. The cobles of Staithes, in a variety of rich colours, sheltered from the open sea on the lee of a harbour wall. At the smaller havens on this cliffbound north-east coast, such sturdy craft might be temporarily out of use, drawn up stern-first on the beach. To me, they resembled exotic seals that had shuffled out of the sea to rest.

Staithes is situated where water in Roxby Beck, tumbling down the stone steps of a wooded glen, is stung by the salty tides. The village hugs the base of the cliffs. The sea smacks its lips against a harbour wall. The most daring building is an inn, aptly named Cod and Lobster. Years ago, when it had been washed into the sea several times, it faced a spring tide and northerly winds that claimed kitchen, scullery, two bedrooms and most of the stock.

Local people cling not only to their property but also to venerable traditions, superstitions and a dialect which had largely faded out elsewhere. Here are some examples of what was common local speech. Eeak was a hook and feeak a length of line without a hook. Clep was a sort of gaff and a brat was a turbot. The names of local properties – Salmon Cottage and Kipper Corner among them - reflect special local interests.

Staithes was a haunted place. Does the headless ghost of the lass who was decapitated by a breakaway lump of Colburn Nab still drift across the little bridge? The ghost of James Harrison, who fell 600-ft to his death at Boulby Cliff, was exorcised by a Catholic priest. Superstition was rife. A fisherman on his way to work in the early morning would return home if he met a woman, a person with cross-eyes or someone with red hair.

Time must not be wasted. Women had far more to do than keep the houses tidy and rear youngsters. Leyland wrote of "blue-eyed, ruddy-skinned, picturesque fisher girls" who "wander along the beach in search of flithers for bait, or trip through the narrow ways and steep courts of the village with baskets of fish poised on their heads, while at the doors sit their elders, in the summer-time, knitting or occupied in the mending of nets."

When fishing was at its most active at Staithes, over fifty cobles would be drawn up in two rows, crowding the beck. Each boat had its team of lads who had been set to work, at a shilling a week, filling sandbags that were used as ballast. The bags were shifted from one side to the other to conform with wind and sailing direction.

Staithes, known locally as "Steers", is best known from its associations with Young James Cook, grocer's assistant, who became the celebrated naval officer and navigator. Cook would have been proud of local lifeboatmen who plucked many a fisherman from the sea. An especially large wave in 1988 overturned the lifeboat. Its design permitted self-righting but, alas, a member of the crew was lost.

A pleasant experience I had in Staithes was a chat with an old lady who was wearing a traditional bonnet. The bonnet-wearing custom was a feature of Whitby and Runswick but endured the longest at Staithes. I was shown such a bonnet, which had a stiffened brim and, at the back, some concealed tape that ensured the bonnet would not be blown away. The whole bonnet might be opened flat for ironing.

Doris Cleverly wrote in 1951: "Like the gay gardens, spotless cottages and the winding paths, the bonnets of Staithes and Runswick Bay are as much part of the lives of these hard-working folk as the sea itself." Older women wore lilac bonnets and the very old favoured black. Bonnets were tied-back if the wearer was searching for bait – for limpets and mussels. It was said of a local girl:

Her bonnet ha' but two ribbons, a-tied

Up under her chin, or let down at the side.

From the air, Runswick, in its little bay, would appear to be even more precariously placed than Staithes. Once, during a major landslip in 1682, the whole village perished with the exception of a single house. Doris Cleverly, a collector of coastal tales, heard in Runswick about the grand sight on Sunday evenings, long ago. On winter nights, fishermen, wearing their best ganseys [jerseys] walked solemnly to church with their lanterns to illuminate the way. The lanterns, still alight, were left near the porch until the end of the service.

The pattern on jerseys was distinctive to the places of origin. The most individual jersey seen by Doris Cleverly had been made at Runswick Bay. Doris recalled: "I met a man wearing one in Staithes and asked if his wife came from Runswick. 'Bye,' he exclaimed. 'How did you know that?'."

I have special memories of Robin Hood's Bay, my destination when following Alfred Wainwright's Coast to Coast Walk. After plodding up hill, down dale, for about a week, beginning by St Bees, on the western shore, it was a joy to quit the out-of-season North York Moors, not yet empurpled with blossom, and stride along a cliff-top with pounding waves far below and the cries of gulls making the air shiver, looking well ahead for a glimpse of the red roofs of Robin Hood's Bay, commonly known as Baytown.

When the compact old part of the village appeared to view, it looked snug behind its lofty concrete seawall. I negotiated a long flight of steps, walked beside a beached boat to the open shore, thence to where a new tide was smacking its lips. There was a ritual to perform. Reaching in a pocket of my haversack for a pebble I had plucked from the shore of the Irish Sea, where my walk had begun, I hurled it into the North Sea. Then, emulating Canute, I let tide lap over my boots, cooling my hot and aching feet.

Over a cup of coffee at the handiest café, I pondered on the name of the place. Had Robin Hood played an important part in local life? It was a long way from Sherwood Forest and no one locally seemed to have a

Staithes. (Yorkshire Post Newspapers)

'Staithes had filled me with so much pleasant expectancy that my first walk down this street of dirty, ugly houses brought me into a querulous frame of mind, and I wondered irritably why the women should all wear lilac-coloured bonnets, when a choice of colour is not difficult.'

Yorkshire, Gordon Home, 1908.

fancy for Lincoln Green. I promptly forgot about Errol Flynn and his Merry Men who featured in legend and an oft-repeated Hollywood film, realising that a more likely connection with Robin Hood related to the Robin Hood Butts, some Bronze Age burial mounds on the moors to the south. They have been associated with Robin Goodfellow, a woodland sprite of medieval folk mythology.

Robin Hood's Bay, or Baytown, sits in the mouth of a ravine overlooking a three-mile-wide bay and with an open landing for boats. John Leyland (1892) asserted that it was the softness of the boulder clay that Bay Town owed most of its characteristic features. "One of the quaintest places imaginable, it hangs in picturesque confusion upon the steep sides of a narrow gully, and upon the very margin of the sea, and fights for dear life, as it were, with the waves, which have often sucked down its seaward dwelling-places into their depths…"

Marie Hartley and Joan Ingilby, celebrated writers about the Yorkshire scene, observed that this place was "shut in by the Ravenscar headland and Ness Point…a series of reefs known as scars jut out into the water. All along this stretch of coast are several little deeply-wooded glens with streams running through them down to the sea, and Baytown is no exception."

In 1816, when fishing was the chief employment of the people, Baytown had five large boats and thirty-five cobles, "but now the young men go to work in the big towns." Three boats were drawn up ready to take visitors rowing. Only one fisherman remained. "The natural life of the place has gone." In recent times, the village has been saved from the North Sea pounding by the aforementioned concrete cliff. It had previously suffered so badly from the decline of inshore fishing that in the 1930s a decayed cliff-edge cottage had a price-tag of about £10. The price zoomed when the wall was in place, giving stability to the village.

Visiting Robin Hood's Bay in the spring, I was temporarily lost in a maze of cobbled streets. A friend living in a building overlooking the sea pointed to windows set at an angle to deflect wave-power in a storm. At Runswick Bay, I saw a thatched coastguard's cottage and cottages that clung to a cliff face with the tenacity shown by house martins when plastering their mud-nests against the likeliest rigid surface.

The first glimpse of each of this trio of North Yorkshire coastal villages had disappointed me. At the clifftop there stood the most modern buildings. For historic character I walked down, down, down, into the parts clustered close to the beaches. A sensitive visitor feels to be walking back in time, mentally enwrapped by a sense of history and tradition. Yet the villages have undergone profound social changes since most of the population were seafaring men, backed up by hard-working women.

What made commercial life tick in those days were lobstering and long-line fishing, with a dash of smuggling. In the 18th century, the Yorkshire coast was the setting for a smuggling trade of vast proportions. It has been estimated that in two and a-half years from 1722 something like 24,353 gallons of spirits were landed between Scarborough and Teesmouth. Smugglers used secret passages. One such hiding place was re-discovered when, in a house half-way up the steps at Robin Hood's Bay, a lady leaned heavily on a wall which collapsed. Beyond, in a passage, were six empty barrels. Several old cottages were linked with a tunnel.

Old-time wreckers lured ships to their doom on savage reefs. The visiting Press Gang enforced an earlier form of National Service. I have already hinted that superstition was rife. It was not completely smothered by Christianity. The folk at Staithes, Runswick and Robin Hood's Bay once looked askance at strangers. If a lad from out of Staithes was seen courting a local lass, he was likely to be "chucked in t'beck." At Staithes, where the tide vents its energy against a harbour wall, it is fascinating to learn of the days when there was a major fishery. The historian Ord noted the interest in cod, haddock and herring in 1846, when over three hundred men were engaged in "this hazardous service." There were upwards of eighty boats, large and small, in constant use during the season.

At the town of Whitby, I heard of spectacular events involving visiting fishermen. One such was the transformation of the harbour towards the end of July by the arrival of the Scottish herring fleet. The season for drift-netting carried on to September. The town saw the arrival of over 140 Scottish boats, some from the far-off Shetlands. Dutch boats tied up at Whitby during the season. The herrings caught were salted down in barrels. At the height of the herring season you might almost walk across the harbour via a succession of fishing boats. At Whitby, it was considered unlucky to wind a ball of wool after sunset:

Thoo tonns thi back ti t'land, and leeaks ti t'sea

As if to show which hest hi sympathy.

As an emissary of *The Dalesman*, who frequently visited the Yorkshire coast, I had become well-acquainted with the writings of Leo Walmsley, "a small shock-headed figure" who was so enthralled by Robin Hood's Bay he renamed it Bramblewick and populated it with fascinating characters. Walmsley's prose has not lost its freshness. A mutual friend recalled him as "a smallish man who carried himself with his head thrown back. His grey hair was thick and wiry, his strong face was tanned and lined by sun and wind. He wore a tweed jacket and grey trousers. On the next meeting between the two, in Cornwall, Leo was wearing a fisherman's woollen jersey, known as a gansey, old trousers and green sea boots."

In his book entitled *So Many Loves*, Leo left us an account of his insight into the temperament of local fishermen. The man he knew as Captain Bunny differed from the others in having a bright personality. Ordinary fishermen regarded their job as a trade. It did not excite them. To Leo, they were "all gruff and gloomy. They would not let you set foot in their cobles or small boats. They didn't mind even boys helping them to haul up the boats in bad weather. Fisherfolk stood, smoking, talking and looking out to sea, or gazing at their cobles, drawn up in rows on the beach."

The Yorkshire coble has long fascinated me. Through many chats with fishermen, I became familiar with this inshore fishing craft, well-suited to the short, sharp seas of the north-east coast. Cobles tugged and fretted at their harbour moorings or, as related, lay idle on a beach, their ancient salty timber absorbing the sun's warmth. At Staithes, a threatened storm stimulated the men to move the cobles on to the staith, where it would be out of harm's way. I heard that the oars of local cobles were fashioned extra strong so that they might be used as skids when the craft was being man-handled up a sloping beach.

The curious name "coble" was anciently rendered kobil, cobil and cobble. A Celtic origin has been suggested, but I could never think of this robust, manly boat as evolving in various stages from the coracle. Cobles, heavy boats in relation to their size, were fashioned of inch-thick planking of larch, with timbers and bottom of English oak. The clinker construction (with overlapping planking on the hull) and the former use of a large lug sail, have closer affinities with another craft of antiquity – the longboat.

A real sailing coble would not hammer or slam in a sea. The forefoot was firm, yet there was enough flare

A gull enjoys the heat rising up through a Staithes chimney stack. (Yorkshire Post Newspapers)

Staithes' outer harbour. (Rod Slater)

above the waterline to lift the head of the boat above any impending wave. In sailing days, a detachable rudder, broad and deep, acted as a keel, ensuring that the boat keeps its stability. The old sailing cobles of the Yorkshire coast had a very deep forefoot and rudder for gripping the water; they had a square stern and were shallow, which gave a fine run for sailing. When the boat was adapted to suit an engine, a deeper stern was needed to immerse the propeller.

During my coastal visits my interest in cobles returned again and again. I admired those I saw and rejoiced in the memories of folk who recalled cobles in their old-time setting of Yorkshire fishing villages, used daily – except on Sunday – by a relatively small number of fishermen, bonded by blood links and a commercial interest in the North Sea. They distributed lobster and crab pots in likely places or deftly cast a long line for cod in the confident hope that the rope would not become ravelled.

In early times, fishing for lobster took place in the summer, from Easter to October, with boats operating in ten fathoms two miles from shore. In the 1960s, fishing methods were revolutionised by the echo-sounder, which could locate subterranean ledges, the best places at which to place lobster pots. Up to the 1950s, long-line fishing went on from October to January, the bait used being mussel. Line and crab fishing was another commercial venture. Lobsters were most numerous nearer the shore. The really big lobsters were in deep water. The keel boat was employed for large fleets of lobster pots. It was not permitted to bring in a berri-ended lobster caught within three miles of the shore. The bait used in lobster and crab pots was gurnard, placed in a "snotter band" in the centre of the pot so that it would be seen.

A lobster pot was made from hazel, with a wooden base. The sides and entry holes were usually hand-knitted with tarred twine. Each pot was connected to the others by a rope about twenty feet long called a tow. Pots were put overhead in a "fleet" of eighty or more, being left underwater during the following night. At the end of each "fleet" was a hummock [skin bowl containing tar] and a start [long stick] running from the centre. There was a flag on top of the stick; the bottom end was weighed with chain or iron.

Cobles aged fifty years and more were still being used when I made my rounds. Some families retained the older methods and traditions. The big new boats meant that much higher expenses were created. If a reasonable living was to be made, daily earnings must average around £20 a day. As my old friend Bill Cowley said: "An old tradition has developed but the men are still the same." The tractor and winch updated coble-fishing. A coble with its engine was somewhat larger than its predecessor. Worthy boats, built in Whitby, had deep drafts and a tunnelled shape for the propeller. They were "beamier" (wider) than the sailing type.

In the Yorkshire fishing story there is a prominent place for the womenfolk. Many years ago, they worked as hard as the men, regularly inspecting rocks and pools on the shore in search of bait. The Staithes lasses prepared lines for the boats and carried these down to the shore in baskets of a flat design. As though that was not enough, women were on hand to transport baskets of fish from boat to home. A testimony to the hard work of fishermen's wives was given me by George Waller, whom I met at Filey. Said George: "These remarkable women had a very hard life by any standards. The work had to be done to eke out a living. When there was a spell of bad weather, and the sea too rough to go fishing, the families only existed."

If a fisherman's wife was going picking on a Monday she would have to be up by four or five o'clock in the morning so she might get the washing done before setting off. It would be dark when she returned home and she would have to start skeining some of the flithers or cracking whelks so that the menfolk could bait the lines." George added: "And women also had care of the children."

My most memorable visit to the North Yorkshire fisherfolk came in October, 1962. I sailed from Whitby with some lobster fishermen. The day began at 2-45am. I sat in a pool of light on the fish quay, drinking hot coffee obtained from an ingenious machine that also retailed hot chocolate and ox-tail soup. Herring gulls screamed and laughed in the darkness.

Soon, it was "whitening up, fast." The words were used by a young fisherman who joined me. A salmon coble passed, heading seaward. Its white hull gleamed in the light. That morning there was a "dead" tide, with no conspicuous movement and a clear reflection, except at the stern of the coble, where Tom Graham, "turned eighty", was plying one of two pairs of oars.

"Queer things, salmon," said the young fisherman as another coble went noiselessly by. "They can smell the rain, you know. They lie at sea waiting for a freshet." He did not care for a freshet. Then the lordly fish would be negotiating the Esk, seeking their spawning grounds. Salmon nets were draped in the sea just outside the claw-like pier extensions.

The first engine to be started belonged to a half-decked coble with a wheelhouse. The sweet, almost sickly fumes of diesel oil clouded the early morning air. Nine other motor cobles, of clinker construction, with high, hollow bow, lay in harbour. Boxes of crab bait – gurnard, minus dorsal fins and tails - were loaded into another coble. The gurnard (or gurnet) has a needle-like spine on its back. If a man's finger is spiked, it painfully festers.

I thumbed a lift in the thirty-year-old keel boat Galilee which, at a steady seven knots, would pick up lobster pots off Staithes and Kettleness. Three fleets of lobster pots – 280 pots in all - had been set out. There was speculation about the number of lobsters and crabs that would be caught. Pointed comments were made about part-timers at the game and the cold spell that kept the catches down. "Them damned lobsters is like tortoises," said one of the crew. "They sleeps when it's cold."

Porpoises were chasing sprats for breakfast. Podgy guillemots rested on the calm water. Fulmars (mallies to the fisherfolk) surveyed a grey sea and grey sky with ancient eyes. At 8-30, the first fishing boats were arriving at the quay, with a goodly quantity of lobsters, crabs and white fish.

Jack Richardson, former lighthouse keeper, added to my knowledge of inshore fishing. He had been on fishing boats operating from Whitby when he was only twelve years of age. His first expedition had been in search of salmon. Nets were lowered from cobles (four nets to each boat, each net being of 100 yards long, sixty meshes deep). For salmon they were floated by flat corks on top and round leads threaded on the bottom rope. As a lad, Jack was paid 9d per stone of salmon landed.

There was poignancy about the way in which he spoke, for inshore fishing at what had been prosperous little villages faded for a variety of reasons. Fishing was chancy. When alternative, dry-land occupations like mining were available, as near Staithes, men found jobs with a secure income. The decline was hastened when the "iron road" of the Scarborough and Whitby railway was laid in the eighteen-eighties.

Overall, fish stocks have been dwindling. Some of the former trawl-areas off the North East Coast are prohibited to commercial fishing in the interests of conservation. In modern times, the money that flows

'The Runswick Bay men are a fine bold race of fishermen; it is said, however, that when they reach the bay with their boats full of glittering fish they never attempt to bring their nets ashore; that charge is left to the wives and mothers of the community, who may be seen toiling along, their heavy-laden baskets on shoulders or on head.'

About Yorkshire, Thomas & Katharine Macquoid, 1894.

The village of Runswick from the beach. (Yorkshire Post Newspapers)

The crew of a Yorkshire coble, circa 1950. (David Joy Collection)

Fishermen attend a coble in the days before tractors did the work. (David Joy Collection)

Women attend a catch of fish at Whitby harbour, circa 1890. (Yorkshire Post Newspapers)

'The fishermen know that the sea is dangerous and the storm terrible, but they have never found these dangers sufficient reason for remaining ashore.'

Vincent Van Gogh

FISHERGIRLS WHITBY · JUDGES' L^TD · 3939.

Looking down on Robin Hood's Bay and a fine view of the coast beyond. (Yorkshire Post Newspapers)

Robin Hood's Bay captured perfectly from the air.
(Yorkshire Post Newspapers)

'Robin Hood's Bay is without question the most picturesque fishing village of Yorkshire, a maze of steep little streets and passages with houses on a diversity of levels. The village does not recommend itself to cars and enjoys the blessings of what the planners now call a pedestrian precinct.'
The Buildings of England – Yorkshire: York and the North Riding, Nikolaus Pevsner, 1966.

Pots await collection at Whitby harbour. (Yorkshire Post Newspapers)

into the villages has been largely generated by tourism and the fact that many of the old buildings have become "second homes" of well-to-do urban folk.

Yet to walk around a former fishing village is still an experience worth having. Houses roofed with red pantiles glow in the sunshine. At nesting time, nesting gulls make the area ring with their calls. And there's usually an old 'un not far away who is happy to talk about "t'long deeard past."

BIRDS OF THE WHITE CLIFFS OF YORKSHIRE

A crescent of chalk across south-east Yorkshire has a spectacular seaward termination in the cliffs of Flamborough, Bempton and Speeton. Follow the cliff-top path, keeping a respectful distance from the edge, and there are places from which you might safely appreciate their size and majesty. Some three miles long and four hundred feet high, the cliffs are tenanted in the nesting season by the largest concentration of sea birds on the English coast. From March until August, bird calls drown all other sounds. Each ledge, each alcove, each bump, hollow and vertical crack has been adapted as a nesting site. Kittiwakes steal the springtime nesting pageant by force of numbers and by the shrillness of their cries. For a short time the nearest colony may be quiet. Then a bird flies in to a noisy and affectionate re-union between mates. All the other birds share in the outburst. Soon, it seems, every cliff echo has been roused by gentle, ocean-going gulls so named from their three-note calls.

I first viewed the kittiwakes of White Cliff Yorkshire in the early 1960s. A cobalt-blue sea contrasted with the brilliance of the chalk, overtopped by clay and thatched with grass and a profusion of wild flowers. The kittiwakes at the nearest nesting sites did not seem to mind me peering at them. I noticed the details of their form and colouring. Small, neat, softly-toned, the kittiwake has a mantle of the gentlest blue-grey, a beak of lemon shade and a manner that is friendly and docile, like a favourite dog. There are some disagreements between birds when the cliff's vacant lots are being filled in spring. One year, I saw two kittiwakes locked together, beak to beak. They were apparently having a trial of strength as they spiralled slowly – rather gracefully, indeed – towards the sea.

Kittiwakes are noisiest during the courtship days. The indentations of the coast form echo-chambers in which their shrill voices resound. They do not seem to rush the task of nest-building. It may be the middle of May before eggs are laid. In Yorkshire there are usually three eggs to a clutch. The average number at colonies further north tends to be smaller. A hungry bird, or one feeding young, dines at sea on fish and shrimps taken from near the surface. One year, when there was a host of small fish swimming inshore at Scarborough, I watched kittiwakes plunge-diving for them like terns. The nesting sites are vacated in August. Birds spend the winter months in the Atlantic. Ringed birds have been recovered from as far afield as Newfoundland.

Bempton, bird life on three miles of sheer cliffs with an elevation of four hundred feet, bombards the senses of visiting naturalists with sights and sounds. A short, sharp sea breaks its back against cliffs that are cracked and seamed, which is ideal for crevice nesting birds like puffins. The musky smell of guano curls over the cliff. When I first visited Bempton cliffs from the village, I motored along a narrow road and parked the car, alongside one or two others, at the edge of a field. Since then the road has been improved, there is a proper car park and, near the cliffs, buildings where information about the place and the birds is dispensed by the Royal Society for the Protection of Birds, who manage the Bempton Cliffs reserve and record up to 45,000 visitors a year.

If you go to Flamborough Head, an eight mile long promontory, with the idea it is a bleak waste of cliffs and coarse grasses, resounding to the roar of the sea and the screams of sea birds, you will be disappointed. Rows of red-roofed bungalows stand in pleasant gardens. Shops and refreshment places cater for locals and visitors. You will become aware of special points of interest such as a chalk tower of 17th century date - the oldest surviving complete lighthouse in the land – and the present imposing lighthouse which is occasionally open for tours.

The praiseworthy action of Bridlington Corporation in buying the headland and thus preserving it from being despoiled came just in time – or perhaps a little late if anything. Flamborough Head has now been designated a Special Area of Conservation. Of the two landing places, North Landing is most popular with photographers. A surprisingly large number of calendar pictures are of a bay flanked by chalk cliffs and so narrow there is no room for second thoughts about navigation. A sea-going man has to be brought up in the place to be comfortable with it. The worst sea comes running in from the north. If it happens that a north-east gale is blowing, it comes straight in!

My happiest moment at North Landing was when I was taken for a cruise in a coble, the inshore fishing boat of the North Yorkshire coast. As we put out to sea, with Richard Emmerson at the tiller and Peter Ellis in support, I half-closed my eyes to protect them from the dazzle on the sunny side of the landing. A trivial piece of information was that on this chalk-cliff coast, diminutive sand martins drill nesting holes into the soft ground between the chalk and the grass.

I sailed in the coble on a day of light wind and high tide. We might safely "hug" the coast. The name of the coble was *Prosperity*. She was directed to Thornwick Bay, to the north, and to the Smugglers' Cave, which has such a large mouth it cannot be overlooked and gives the impression that the cliff is yawning. We entered a shallow inlet containing the pinnacle known as the Queen Rock. Once there was a King Rock. Local folk will tell you that King Rock collapsed about the time that George VI died. It's probably not quite true… With the engine "ticking over" we cruised near the high cliffs which had terraces packed with guillemots. More guillemots were on shelving rocks close to the sea. They dived into the waves and departed under water at speed. I heard the metallic calls of jackdaws. Herring gulls gave laughing cries as though responding to a doubtful joke.

"Little Denmark" is the name given to this part of the district. The Danes are said to have introduced a crop of words and expressions to Flamborough. They are also credited with the local version of the Sword Dance, in which eight men make a frame. There are two players and two beggars. Even the Danes, worshippers of Thor and Odin, could not have been more superstitious than the folk of Flamborough. I was introduced to many of them by Mr and Mrs Tant Cross, who straightway admitted that they have little control over people's behaviour today.

In Old Flamborough, no-one would walk over the top of the fishing lines when they were being hauled out. If you wanted to see a local fisherman's face drop, mention "pig", a word that also influenced the facial expressions of women. A lady who had died at Flamborough a month before my visit in 1955 was so superstitious that pigs, rabbits and eggs were not to be mentioned in her presence. A parson in a silk hat was a symbol of bad luck. A fisherman who saw such a hat would promptly say: "Oh, laws, drum's up – we sall

Guillemots and Kittiwakes. (W.R. Mitchell)

Birdlife at Bempton. (W.R. Mitchell)

ev nea mare good luck this week."

Mrs Cross told me that her mother used to go down the cliffs for fishing bait. "At the bottom of a cliff there was a hole in a rock that gave access to another little bay. It was the only way of getting through. One day, a fat man went down with the women and on his return he stuck fast in the hole. The women were in danger of drowning, for the tide was rising fast. Fortunately, they managed to remove his jacket and get him clear of the hole.

At Flamborough Head, I enjoy sitting by the clifftop path, near a bank of gorse, especially in springtime when it bears yellow blossom – and the cliff-nesting birds are vocal. The white buildings of lighthouse and foghorn, squat and tidy, look from a distance like outcrops. For the Flamborough folk of centuries ago, the past was not peaceful for long. Apart from the constant battle with nature, and that early trouble with the Danes, there is a stirring tale of John Paul Jones, American adventurer. In a sea battle off Flamborough Head in 1779, his ship was put to flight.

The bravest men at Flamborough and Bempton were the cliff-climmers. They descended the cliffs on ropes rather than climbing them as the unofficial title implied. Their activity was not for bravado or as entertainment but to gather seabirds and eggs for sale. A cliff-climmer needed strong nerves, a body-line two hundred feet long, with harness, and a thinner safety line. Four men comprised a party "with one of them down and three up". Lowered over the cliff, he was soon out of sight of those on top, dangling like a spider and using the footwork of a First Division footballer on his way from ledge to ledge, canvas bags for the loot being attached to his body. A good climmer collected from sixty and eighty guillemot eggs at a drop. It had a drastic effect on the bird population. A local man gave another reason for an increasing scarcity of auks: "Kittiwakes is driving 'em out…"

Land and sea mean that in this part of Yorkshire a farmer and a fisherman are working friends. Inland, on a visit to the White Cliffs, I saw a farmer on a red tractor attached to a plough that was breaking up the heavy soil. Seawards, a Flamborough coble was hove-to while the crew dumped lobster pots into the sea. As I resumed my walk, following a path that seemed to have an aversion to going straight, seabirds came to view. The cliffs were festooned by kittiwakes. Fulmars glided noiselessly by, gazing at me with their cold northern eyes. Razorbills laid their eggs – one per bird – in a crevice in bare rock.

At nearby Bempton Cliffs I saw a congregation of over 200,000 seabirds. Ledges were packed with guillemots, currently up to 60,000 and their chicks. Into view came a portly little puffin, with its smart plumage, black and white like a dress suit, its eyes blinking over its parrot-like beak. From that moment I developed a passion for the puffins that in Yorkshire are spread thinly, nesting in cracks and crannies. My first live puffin looked like a bumble bee against the sea-glare. A small, rotund body was supported by short wings that were being worked so quickly they were just a blur. I fancied that if they had stopped beating for an instant, the bird would have dropped from the sky.

Pictured in colour in a bird book, the puffin looks as large and imposing as a penguin. Even then, flicking through my first bird book, I recognised the puffin as something special in the bird world. I was captivated by the triangular beak – tinted red, yellow and blue, like the false nose donned by a clown. This is adapted for holding fish, a dozen at a time. It saves energy by carrying a number of sand-eels and other small stuff from sea to the nestlings. The bill is also a status symbol, proclaiming seniority. Horny patches are grown for the nesting season, then jettisoned for the winter, changing in size and appearance with each succeeding springtime.

That day I had followed a cliff-edge footpath from North Landing. A blue-ganseyed fisherman mentioned his first close encounter with the puffin. Said he: "It nests in holes among rocks. I put my hand into a hole, looking for an egg. All I got for my pains was a nip from its neb [beak]. And what a nip! It made my eyes water…"Another fisherman said: "We had a stuffed puffin in a glass case till my mother got fed up of dusting it." The puffin looks cuddly but is not cuddlesome, except in its soft-toy form. In real life, this bird is one of nature's "toughies", able to fend for itself.

In future years, the sight of my first puffin was to come to mind at the start of each new bird carnival on the Yorkshire coast. I have mentioned cliff-climmin. In earlier times, the seabirds of Flamborough and Bempton were not permitted to nest in peace. A directory of 1831 referred matter-of-factly, without sense of guilt, to raids on eggs and even adult birds. The eggs, with what seemed like an endless variety of colouring, were collected in bushels and transported to the "sugar house" at Hull. Some were sold to housewives and visitors. Men with leisure and sporty inclinations brought shotguns to the cliff sides in spring and probably laughed loudly as they fired into the densely-packed colonies of birds. The poorest shot could be guaranteed a kill. Victorian times saw a boom in feathered hats for ladies. Kittiwakes were slain in their thousands so their feathers could meet the demand for such an adornment.

Spanning the Victorian shooting craze, and long outliving it, was the aforementioned business of cliff-climmin. After my initial interviews with some of them, I gathered more detail of the climmer's world. Several gangs of climbers operated during the early part of the nesting season, dividing the cliffs among themselves. None of them would dream of trespassing on another's terrain. There were four men in a gang – a climber and three friends who operated at the cliff top. An iron stake with a running pullet at the top was firmly driven in to the cliff edge and a guide rope fastened to it, the black being thrown over the cliff. Precautions against the chafing of the rope were taken.

A climmer's rope was about three hundred feet long. The climmer donned a harness consisting of loops of flat rope with an attached belt that buckled round his belt. Baskets to collect eggs, mainly those of the auks. Some eggs were destined to be blown and cocooned in cotton wool, neatly arranged in the cabinets of the collectors. Others were taken to butchers and fish merchants, who arranged them in their windows, hoping to attract attention to their real wares. Most of the eggs were cooked and eaten locally. For over two hundred years the cliff-climmers undertook their dangerous occupation and the seabirds heard the rasp of well-shod boots on the ledges or made off hurriedly as minor falls of clay and stones heralded the approach of humans who protected their own heads by filling bowler hats with grass. Some climmers donned policeman-type helmets or (after the Great War) the Army steel helmet.

Two pieces of legislation ended the depletion of the Yorkshire seabird stock. Professor Alfred Newton, addressing the British Association for the Advancement of Science in 1868, condemned the shooting of birds at Flamborough Head. On February 26, 1869, Mr Christopher Sykes, the second son of Sir Tatton Sykes of Sledmere and MP for the East Riding, outlined the Sea Birds Preservation Act to the House of Commons. At the second reading of the Bill, sponsored by Mr Sykes, Mr Clay (MP for Hull) and Mr Ward Jackson (MP for Hartlepool) an amendment extending the protection not only for the birds but also their eggs was carried.

All puffin
species have
predominantly
black or black
and white
plumage, and
large beaks.
(W.R. Mitchell)

Gannets. A bird of 'regal flight'. (W.R. Mitchell)

Herring Gulls at Bempton. (W.R. Mitchell)

In the House of Lords debate, the Duke of Richmond reminded their Lordships that large numbers of people went down in the breeding season by excursion trains for the sole purpose of shooting the sea birds at their breeding sites. The Archbishop of York asserted that many birds were shot for the sale of their plumage to adorn ladies' hats.

Following the Lords' Debate on May 4, 1869, the Bill progressed rapidly. It received the Royal Assent on June 24 of that year. In 1974 further legislation ended the two centuries-old pastime of "cliff-climmin". The centenary of the 1869 legislation was fittingly marked on a sunny March day when I was invited to join a special cruise in the *Corona* from Scarborough to the Bempton cliffs. To the north of the chalk zone we saw cormorants hanging out their wings to dry as they perched on coloured cliffs. A fulmar glided silently by. Small groups of auks scuttered away from our vessel when it was almost upon them. An hour and a half out of Scarborough, when it was almost high tide, and the chalk cliffs of Flamborough Head were in shadow, we cruised slowly near the awesome Bempton cliffs.

Several puffins twisted their heads as they breasted the waves. I expected to see far more guillemots on the water but they were either out at sea or perched in their thousands on the ledges, looking like two-tone skittles. This was March, a time when auks are most conspicuous in the air and on the water. Kittiwakes whirled in the air like snowflakes but few sounds reached us on the boat. It was like watching a film with a missing soundtrack.

Most of our attention was given to the gannets which had begun the colonisation on the broader, erstwhile guillemot ledges. I had seen thousands of gannets at their nests on Ailsa Craig and Bass Rock, solitary rocks on either side of Scotland. Now I was watching Yorkshire gannets, which took flight, soaring on wings with a six feet span. One of them soared, turned, circled, then dipped close to the sea and moved off only feet above it with no conspicuous flapping of wings. The *Corona* made two passes at the cliffs; then we headed back for Scarborough where Athol Wallis, one of the principal organisers of the cruise, described it as "a historic occasion."

I returned to the Yorkshire gannetry on a chilly evening in 1974. Having glanced through old copies of *The Dalesman*, which I was to edit for many years, I had been enthralled by an account written by a friend, A. Norman Handley, recalling an evening spent with naturalist friends at Bempton during the first week of June, 1948. Driving rain was falling in Filey Bay. Forked lightning was almost continuous at sea. The roaring of the sea and calling of thousands of seabirds was deafening.

At Jubilee Corner, a few of the birds dwarfed other avian residents in size and splendour. They "stood out like leading actors on a stage, though no stage ever approached this for scenic grandeur — a grandeur made awe-inspiring by the approaching storm." Norman saw five gannets, "magnificent creatures." Only one was nesting. It was sitting on the only gannet's egg to be found in all England! A gannet rose and circled and settled once again. Norman and his friends ran before the breaking storm, which "fell as a curtain blotting out the final act of an amazing scene."

Some of the older gannets inspected the nesting cliffs as early as January. On my springtime visit, weather conditions were tolerable to within a few yards of the edge of Bempton Cliffs. I found a safe place from which to gaze at gannets. The blast hitting the cliffs was turbulent and damp. In my ears was the seabird chorus, sustained by thousands of ocean-going kittiwakes. Gutteral calls came from guillemot and gannet.

The stench of massed birds tainted the wind. Some of the gannets straddled heaps of nests that, cemented by the birds' excrement, were festooned by oddments of fishing net. Young gannets were at various stages of development, having gone through the "powder-puff" stage when they were copiously swaddled in down, to the feathering-up stage, the new feathers being brown-black. Not for four years would the birds eventually moult out of the last traces of the dark juvenile plumage to become showy adults.

Adult gannets and young birds at various stages of maturity sailed the air currents. The darkly-plumaged young looked larger than the adults. From maybe twenty feet, I admired the regal flight of an adult, as evidenced by its white plumage with sharply contrasting black wing tips. The bird's cigar-shaped body created no drag. I was close enough to this gannet to see its yellow eye and straw-yellow head. A young gannet leaves a ledge at Bempton after about ninety days, leaping into the wind, fluttering to the sea which it will not be able to leave until it has lost some weight.

The White Cliffs of Yorkshire look durable, but each year there are subtle changes brought about by weathering and the force of the tides. Sometimes, the transformation is spectacular, as when a lightning bolt struck a buttress on the cliffs of Flamborough Head in August, 2006. A vast amount of rock fell into the sea. There is more to this striking white coastline than nesting seabirds. Flamborough, protruding far to sea, is attractive to many bird migrants in autumn and therefore to a host of ornithologists who, with binoculars at the ready, excitedly note the offshore passage of seabirds.

Climmers at work. Their practice was banned in 1954. (Yorkshire Post Newspapers)

Port Mulgrave – James Booth (1867 - 1953) (collection of Mr & Mrs Gordon Hancock)

DAVID JOY

The Lost Port

David Joy, MBE, is a former editor of *The Dalesman* and has written extensively on many aspects of Yorkshire. A former chairman of North Yorkshire Branch of CPRE (Campaign to Protect Rural England), he has had a lifelong interest in preservation of the countryside and the well being of its traditional farming. He received the MBE for 'services to the environment in the North East'.

He here recalls a visit to Port Mulgrave and its harbour situated between Staithes and Runswick Bay. Built to facilitate the transportation of iron ore from the nearby mineworkings the port is now abandoned, but it has an interesting history and a curious atmosphere. Although access can be tricky, visiting its remains is worth the effort if the weather is with you.

Port Mulgrave still clung to the Yorkshire coast with the tenacity of a limpet, yet it would be only a matter of time before it vanished for ever into a very watery grave. Ironstone mines, which had provided the sole excuse for its existence, were long defunct. The harbour, deprived of a reason for survival and abandoned by mankind, was slowly being tortured to death by the relentless North Sea waves.

Such was reputedly the case when I headed towards lonely Port Mulgrave, between Staithes and Runswick Bay, on a cold and grey afternoon way back in February 1966. Could it possibly be as bleak as this reputation suggested?

It proved to be much worse. The road stopped abruptly at the cliff edge, where the wind seemed to be coming straight from the Arctic hell-bent on freezing every living thing into a permanent feature of the coastline. Way below, waves were in fury everywhere except at the remains of the port, which resembled two giant work-worn fingers poking their way into an enormous bowl of dirty grey washing-up water.

Thoughts of following in Masefield's footsteps and going down to the sea again were quickly abandoned. It would not have been a journey of love but rather of folly to descend to what looked like a dreary, storm-battered cove. I retreated to a deserted Staithes and spent the night in a room close enough to the sea for a howling wind to blow salt spray through the window. It counted for nothing that the four nearby houses were hopefully named 'Harbour View', 'Beach View', 'Sea View' and 'Ocean View'! It suggested an ever more distant horizon, but not even the harbour was visible through the gale.

Few places can equal the Yorkshire coast for rapid weather transformation. Next morning a brilliant sun pierced through the curtains and woke me at an almost heathen hour. I decided to forego breakfast and get out of doors at once. This was the North Sea, not the then musically fashionable South Pacific, yet somehow Port Mulgrave like Bali-Hai was exerting a compelling urge to go back. Fuelled by the imagination, the return journey seemed to take no time at all.

It was hard to visualise this was the same place that had seemed so depressing little more than twelve hours previously. Onshore lighting was carving up the still swollen sea into myriads of brilliantly coloured pools. Half of Europe was just over the horizon and to the north-west the Cleveland Hills were clothed in an early morning pink and purple haze. The only sound was coming from a tractor methodically ploughing some vast field and followed by scores of wheeling seagulls.

This time there could be no question of staying on the cliff top. Yet I knew that a descent was easier said than done. I had been forewarned that the harbour could make a strong claim to be the most inaccessible in the whole of Britain. It was said that, even in dry weather, only the sure-footed and supremely energetic should make an attempt to get there. Above all, they needed to remember they had also to get back!

In today's terminology the descent is less than a hundred metres, but in those days it was expressed as some three hundred feet – and that sounded infinitely worse. To say the least, I found the apology for a track more than a touch disconcerting. It made no concessions to being engineered, wth long and almost level stretches followed by sudden precipitous drops. All the way down jagged stones formed a hazard for feet that could so easily meander with such tempting views to distract the eyes. Some bits were not as stony as others, but this was only because a covering of clay had turned to a treacherous ooze following the previous day's downpour.

The path descended in zig-zags, although there were short cuts for anyone with the agility of a mountain goat. Somehow reaching the bottom without injury, I had my first close look at Port Mulgrave. It was without any doubt absolutely 'away from it all'. Of the two harbour walls bravely reaching out into the sea, that on the north side had recently been breached by a tremendous storm and reduced almost to its foundations. The south wall was badly battered but still survived sufficiently to provide shelter for three cobles – the local name for small fishing boats.

To my surprise I was not the only human there that morning. Standing on the edge of the pier and contemplating his surroundings with a minimum of movement was a sea angler. In true Yorkshire fashion, we did not speak to each other. He had been there first and I sensed that he, like me, was disappointed not to have the place to himself. So I crept away as stealthily as possible, hoping the sound of my footfall had not sent all the fish scurrying round to Runswick Bay for the day.

It was clearly time for quiet reflection, first gazing out to sea and conjuring up an era long past. Once the waters would have been alive with sailing ships, their skippers no doubt all too conscious of a double whammy. The East Coast not only held the record for the largest number of sea disasters round the British Isles but the worst section of all was the passage from the Tees past Port Mulgrave to Flamborough Head. What the North Sea lacked in size it made up for in ferocity, and when a north-easterly gale was blowing there were few places more hostile to man.

The skipper of a sailing ship caught in such a storm was faced with a near impossible choice. He had to decide whether to try and ride out the storm or take the near suicidal step of attempting to gain one of the small harbours such as Port Mulgrave. The outcome was usually disaster on an unimaginable scale, with almost a thousand ships sometimes being wrecked off the East Coast in a single year. As I mused on past

Port Mulgrave, photographed by the writer at the time of his memorable visit in February 1966. The bricked-up mouth of the tunnel, through which travelled the lifeblood for the port, can be seen at the extreme right. (David Joy Collection)

tragedies, I could not help noticing two masts of a submerged boat sticking out of the harbour and wondering what sorry saga might have occurred.

Still staring out to sea, I thought also of the small boats that would once slip into Port Mulgrave under cover of darkness in the hope they would be noticed by no one – and especially not by excise men. Smuggling was rife along this stretch of coast for 150 infamous years beginning around 1700. It was all too tempting at a time when tea bought in Holland at seven pence a pound undercut the English retail price by almost two-thirds. There were similar margins on tobacco and gin.

Typical of the times was the occasion when smugglers landed no less than 500 tubs of gin close to the now demolished Old Mulgrave Castle Inn. Excise men had been tipped off, eventually finding half the cargo and loading it into a cart. They set off towards Whitby, but at Sandsend a hostile crowd gathered and a linchpin was pulled off an axle. The cart tilted sideways and liquor promptly poured into the gutter from the upset tubs. It was eagerly scooped up by the crowd, some of whom used their boots for the purpose!

It may have seemed good stirring stuff, but there was a nastier side to the glory days of smuggling. The men could be cruel and violent and by the 1770s smuggling in the area either side of Port Mulgrave had reached a dreadful peak. Armed gangs roamed the neighbourhood, setting fire to farms, slaughtering cattle and

A sign points the way to the site of the ruined harbour at Port Mulgrave –
even in good weather it can be a lonely and inhospitable walk. (Rod Slater)

Long and Short Row, Port Mulgrave. These houses would once have housed miners and their families. Interestingly their front doors and gardens face inland; their back doors face out to sea. (Rod Slater)

kidnapping women. Villagers were in constant fear of their lives and appealed for troops to be brought in for their protection.

I could have continued staring seawards and reflecting on those days for eternity. Yet much as Port Mulgrave, tucked away at the foot of high cliffs, might seem a smugglers' paradise, I knew that this was not the prime reason for its existence. In truth this was even more bizarre and the clue was a bricked-up tunnel mouth in of all places part way up the cliff. It looked utterly incongruous but without it the port would never have existed.

The saga began in the mid-nineteenth century, when deposits of iron ore were being worked in the Staithes area. Walter White in his classic 1858 book, *A Month in Yorkshire,* described his visit to the village and how he met "a few sturdy fellows striding past, yellow from head to foot with a thick ochre-like dust". They had come from the ironstone diggings.

The workings became centred in the valley of Roxby Beck to the south-west of Staithes, but development was hindered by the lack of any easy way of moving the ore out of the deep defile. Matters were transformed by the arrival on the scene of Sir Charles Mark Palmer, MP, an eminent shipbuilder and ironmaster. He was not a man to be troubled by such difficulties and moreover had the necessary resources to overcome them.

Leasing the mineral rights from the Earl of Mulgrave, he boldly drove a mile-long tunnel out of the valley and laid a railway through it to carry tubs of ore to the coast. The tracks emerged straight out of the cliff onto a gantry rising above the main sea wall of the harbour he audaciously created. Built where nothing man-made had previously dared to exist, it took its name from that of the landowner. There were after all associations with ancient history, as 'Mulgrave' comes from old Norse with 'muli' meaning a headland or crag and 'gryfna' a pit or hollow. Perhaps also it was a case that Port Palmer might just have been a shade too much!

The whole enterprise cost the then immense sum of £40,000, but it proved to be money well spent. At the harbour a beam engine powered an endless rope that brought the tubs of ore through the tunnel as required. At each high tide the port became a hive of feverish activity as ore was tipped from the gantry into sailing barges, which were soon conveying some 3,000 tons per week to the Palmer shipbuilding and iron furnaces at Jarrow. By 1870 these had been replaced by a series of paddle tugs and lighters, which in turn gave way two decades later to steamers bestowed with such familiar local names as *Staithes, Runswick* and *Loftus.*

All went well until the First World War when the mines and hence the port went into decline. The depression of the 1920s reduced production to an increasingly erratic basis, although even after closure in 1930 a skeleton staff continued to be employed in the hope of revival. It was destined not to happen and in 1935 the harbour was finally abandoned, although not without one last fight. During the salvage operations a fierce fire broke out from some unknown cause as the massive gantry was being dismantled, resulting in its almost complete destruction. Its stone buttress walls soon became occupied by fishermen's huts, and the concrete slab floors of the boilers and engine house proved ideal for stacking crab pots.

No matter how fascinating the history, staring at a bricked-up tunnel mouth has its inspirational limitations. It was time to begin the long and tedious ascent back to the cliff top. After twenty minutes and six rests I made it, heart beating feverishly, knees quaking and brow sweating. Nothing would have induced me to make such a climb again that day.

By now folk were stirring in the scattered community set back from the cliff edge and I was able to learn more of times still distantly remembered by those in the teatime of life.

The miners were not universally revered and I was told that they were "a wild lot, prone to fighting". Instead of receiving a welcome, a stranger could expect to be met with a shower of stones and a tirade of abuse to send him on his way.

Yet I was also shown a copy of the Reverend Atkinson's *History of Cleveland*, which presented a different picture: "The number of men and boys employed at these works averages about three hundred and fifty, and their character and conduct is spoken of as generally good."

Perhaps this was simply a member of the clergy taking a charitable view, as he also went out of his way to praise the actions of their employers: "The company is spoken of as having built more houses lately for the use of their people, which are larger than those of older date and contain more conveniences than the usual miners' cottages, and many of which have gardens and pig-cotes attached to them." No doubt the delicious smell of freshly-cooked, home-cured bacon was all-important to miners coming off a long and gruelling shift.

The miners' houses are still there. They were built in an 'L' formation, and without overstretching the imagination were named Long Row and Short Row. Some county official eventually decided that both rows would sound more pleasant if renamed Rosedale Lane, but it made not a jot of difference to most of the inhabitants and merely created confusion. Such difficulties did not apply to two very different houses standing on their own and more akin to large villas. One was built for use by the Palmers when visiting Port Mulgrave and the other was the mine manager's house. Equally curious in its way was a block of flats, originally constructed by the ironstone company as a dormitory for single men working in the mines.

It was time to move on, but I could not resist one long, last look at the lonely yet valiant port. Some words in that classic seafaring book, *Brief Glory*, came back to me: "As the current carries the 'Dewdrop' into what would have been, when I last saw it, a busy and crammed-full port, I beheld desolation. No little pointsman in uniform with the dark-shadowed eyes, no ship-chandler or Puddin-rice shop. I steered my boat over water full of shadows, until my bowsprit almost touched the bridge, and here I moored, feeling like an intruder in some hallowed graveyard and wanting to speak in whispers.

"A few days only did I linger in the uncanny stillness. After visiting a few well-remembered spots, I fled, fled as fast as wind could speed me; nor did I ever re-visit the old, derelict port in any ship, large or small."

I too now fled and have never visited Port Mulgrave again. Today, over forty years later, the harbour has virtually been swept away but the area is probably busier than ever. More and more walkers pound the Cleveland Way along the cliff top, and ever-increasing numbers go down to the sea at low tide in search of fossils as well as the anemones and lichens that abound in rock pools. Yet somehow I know that nothing will recapture the magic of that first visit. Port Mulgrave is now truly the lost port.

A blustery day on the beach, the Abbey provides a stunning backdrop in this image. (Yorkshire Post Newspapers)

R.J. ELLORY

Whitby: Hidden History

R.J. Ellory was born in Birmingham. He is one of the most celebrated crime and thriller writers in the United Kingdom and his books have gained a worldwide reputation. His novel *A Quiet Belief in Angels* was a Richard and Judy Book Club choice and has since become an international bestseller. His latest novels are *The Anniversary Man* and *The Saints of New York*. His books have been shortlisted for and awarded several prizes, and are now available in twenty-five languages. For more information visit www.rjellory.com

R.J. Ellory visited Whitby on a book promotional tour and fell in love with the town. He here presents his personal homage to the history and character of this inspirational seaport.

There are places where history hides.

Where chambers and catacombs and corridors of stone drop deep into the earth; where footworn risers walk deep beneath the surface, and with each new step we reveal a moment of time otherwise forgotten, lost, voiceless.

Not so here.

There are places where history hides.

Where the tumbled arch of majestic edifice lies buried and broken, or scattered and stolen, where Nature has sought to reclaim all that was hers and bring it home for ever.

Not so here.

There are places where history hides.

Where the challenge of tide and time have proven too great, and the once-immutable landmarks of passage and progress have ached and strained beneath the pressure of decades, even centuries, and we are witness to little more than a vague disturbance in the soil; an echo of footsteps long-gone and silent.

Not so here.

For there are places where history breathes, and the sound of that breathing is both the past and the future together, and they coincide in the present and stand as testimony to all that was, all that is, and all that shall be.

So shall you find us here.

We are the mouth of the river.

We are carved from the land by the sea.

We are ancient, as old as all things, and we have been here forever.

We are King Oswy, standing firm against the might of Penda, pagan king of Mercia, his forces greatly outnumbered, his people ravaged, his hands clasped together in prayer. 'Give me victory O Lord,' he pleads, 'and I shall consecrate my daughter to your service, my lands to your works,' and so it was. Penda and his nobles walked out to battle, and were slain, and Oswy honoured his vow to God, twelve estates of ten hides each to be given over to the founding of monasteries.

And as we take our name, as this founding settlement becomes known as Streonshalh, we are witness to Ælflæda, daughter of Oswy, fulfilling her father's pledge and dedicating her life to Christ. And amongst us is Hilda, here now as first Abbess, and the poet Cædmon, and all who resided here and found learning and culture and wisdom and faith.

And then amongst us too are the hordes from Scandinavia, the Danes who crossed Raven's Hill and burst upon the land as if the very floodgates of Hell had been opened. Sacking, burning, killing, tearing all asunder, and blood was spilled upon this land, and tears were shed, and the monastery was torn to the ground and scattered to the winds in flames and smoke as black as jet.

And faith was silent, and wisdom lost, and Cædmon's words were memories in a breeze that crept through the fallen ruins of what was once so proud.

'We are not forgotten.' Such words as these were heard in this breeze. 'We will return.'

Two hundred years, and still we stand above the sea and bear witness to the past. The future greets us, and with St. Peter and St. Hilda carrying our faith, with Regenfrith - monk soldier and dutiful captain of William de Percy – beside us, we bear the stones upon our backs and we rebuild, we return this land to the service of God and open these doors once more. There is sanctuary here. We are known as Presteby; this habitation of priests.

And then we find our new name, which is Hwytby, a heritage that will echo through the centuries to come, and still a thousand years hence, a thousand years again, and will stand for all who walked here, and the vow that was made.

We are Whitby.

So shall you find us.

We do not hide our history here.

We grow. We track our way inland. We are West Cliff and the Haggerlythe. We are the Church Stairs and Cædmon's Trod. We are oak ships built by the hands of fathers and sons, brothers and neighbours. We are whaling vessels surging forward against the coming tide, travelling out to the same lands from whence the hordes of savages came to steal our homes and hearths. We are Captain James Cook, his apprenticeship, his teacher, his second home. We are captain of the coal vessel, Freelove, plying a trade between London and the Tyne. And it was from here we became a Master and Commander for Kings and Queens alike, a man of the Seven Years' War, of the Siege of Quebec, of Newfoundland, of the Pacific. 'I intend not only to go farther than any man has been before me, but as far as I think it is possible for a man to go.' Such were his words. He journeyed so that the world would be carried to our door, and the journey was conceived in Whitby.

We do not hide our history here.

We are jet, now gathered from these very shores. We are as black as night, but we shine like diamonds. We are the mourning jewels of Queen Victoria. We are gifts and dowries. We are treasure.

We are the lives lost at sea. We are the hospital ship Rohilla, the disaster of nineteen fourteen. We are the eighty-five drowned at sea, our bodies now buried here in the churchyard. We are the signal post at the end of the headland, shelled by the German battleships, Von der Tann and Derfflinger. We are the Abbey, once again battered and bruised and beaten down by enemy fire. But still we stand, and still we look down upon the sea.

We are the sunset over Kettleness, we are the moors and Mulgrave Castle. We are the one hundred and ninety-nine steps, and that indefinable, breathless, wide-eyed moment as we stand at the top and look away towards the water and see the world disappear before us.

We are the narrow streets and tall houses, the symmetry of roofs and chimneys. We are the cormorants and gulls. We are the landmark from the water, the safe haven, the welcome home.

And we do not hide our history here.

I am a stranger, but I am familiar. I smell the sea. I smell the salt-air. I breathe in this place, and I feel it breathing back. It is cold, and as I turn my collar against the wind, as I bury my hands in my pockets and watch the sails vanish over the horizon, I think of those who have stood before me, here in these self-same hills, and I am in awe. There is a quiet and resolute strength in the faces of these people, a strength that has perhaps passed from generation to generation down through the centuries. We have been here all along, those faces say, and we will always be here.

I climb one hundred and ninety-nine steps. I look out across the bay. I see the piers, the ships, the narrow craft, the dinghies. I see the brightly-coloured coats and hats of tourists. I see how the present has attempted a quiet invasion. And yet I see it all vanish before me, as if the real truth of this place is always here, just beneath the surface, no deeper than a fingerprint.

The Abbey stands in ruins, but its silhouette against the sky tells me more than any book or travelogue or anecdote. Thirteen hundred years have elapsed since first a stone was laid by King Oswy, honouring his promise, fulfilling his vow. Thirteen hundred years. Fifty generations of change and progress, of war and peace, of families and friends, of feuds and fellowships. This is so much our England, the England of Kings and Queens, of saints and martyrs, of mighty battles, of men fallen and forgotten on this very soil. Forgotten by all but Whitby itself, for the sound of their voices and the hammer of their footsteps still echoes deep in the foundations of this land.

'Whitby is delightful in three ways at least: for the abbey, which, as a ruin, is sublime as well as picturesque; for the parish church, the like of which is not to be found anywhere in the country; and for the busy quaysides with the long irregular rows of houses, picturesque in so different a way from the picturesqueness of the abbey.'

The Buildings of England —Yorkshire the North Riding, Nikolaus Pevsner, 1966

The whole of this famous and influential town as seen from the air. (Yorkshire Post Newspapers)

I am grateful for solitude, for altitude, for the air I breathe as I look out over Whitby and try to fathom its past.

I see now what Abraham Stoker saw. He was a writer, as am I, and I appreciate the depth and profundity of emotional impact a single place, a single moment can have. He saw the *Demeter* entering the harbour. He – and only he – knew the nature of its dark cargo. He created a legend that is now part of our collective history – a legend harking back to Vlad the Impaler, to Nosferatu, and thence to Dracula - and it was here that he created it. Now, more than a hundred years old, that legend is as alive as it ever was.

And Lewis Carroll, Elizabeth Gaskell, Wilkie Collins - they all came here, and they found their inspiration in these narrow streets, along these piers, and through these circuitous walkways.

Whitby is a jewel of many facets. Light and shade, brilliance and shadow; they reside as neighbours, and here we see that one is nothing less than complemented by the other. I see this jewel with the eyes of the traveller, the visitor, the transient. And I am seen in return with a rare and curious gaze that is at once hospitable, and yet somehow distant. You are welcome here, it says, but you are not one of us. We will care for you, we will make our hearths and homes yours for as long as you reside, but you will leave, and we wish you well for your departure. Return and you will find us still here, living the lives we have always led, and we will welcome you once more. But remember this: However many times you come, you will always be a traveller, a visitor, a transient. You will never see the history of this town the way that we see it. You will never truly grasp the loyalty we feel for this, our home.

Perhaps it is the sea. Perhaps, so close to the might of Nature, our human vulnerability and brevity is appreciated. There are memories out there too. The drowned, the lost, the vanished, the missing. Men and women killed in battle, in storms; those drawn into the lightless depths by tides and currents too strong to be resisted; the fishermen, the whalers, the able seamen rendered so desperately unable by the power of the ocean. It is all here, and it waits.

Yes, perhaps it is the sea, a constant reminder of our own fallibility and impermanence. A constant reminder that however old we may be, and however long we have been here, we are nothing but infants in comparison.

I descend the Church Stairs. Gravity assists me this time. I turn and look back at the silhouette of the Abbey and feel the tug of something. The mystery of the past is impenetrable. We will never really know. No-one remains to tell us what really happened as the Vikings came, as Henry VIII ordered the destruction of the Abbey in 1540, as Thomas Chaloner of York defied the Vatican's monopoly and established his own alum mines here, as the first whaling ship crossed the horizon in 1753. No-one can tell us, but there is something in the air, something in the ground beneath my feet, that makes me believe I can understand some small part of it. At least that.

I am neither Bram Stoker nor Gaskell, nor Carroll nor Collins, but I am a writer, and I see with a writer's eyes, and I hear with a writer's ears, and the sound of the gulls and the cormorants, the breath of the tide as it ebbs and flows, the sound of the wind as it carries salt from the ocean and makes its way along the narrow streets…these things have always been the same. These are the things that do not change. I see them just as they were seen. I hear them just as they were heard. I watch the same sun as it sets over Kettleness, and I know that this sun will sink below the horizon time and time again, and again long after I am gone.

Caedmon's Cross.
Created in honour of
'the father of English
Sacred Song. Fell
asleep hard by, 680'.
(Rod Slater)

East Cliff and St Mary's Church from the harbour. (Rod Slater)

Mouth of the harbour with trawler leaving. (Rod Slater)

'It is perhaps a consequence of long-continued isolation that Whitby and its inhabitants are still so primitive, and set such an unlimited value on the importance and beauty of their town and its surroundings.'

About Yorkshire, Thomas & Katharine Macquoid, 1894.

The replica of Captain Cook's HMS Endeavour enters Whitby Harbour. The ship was built by local craftsmen over a 12 month period between 2001/02. Based on original maritime drawings it is approximately 40% of the ship's original size. It is situated at Whitby harbour and makes regular voyages around the coast. (Yorkshire Post Newspapers)

Perhaps, as a stranger, I am blessed. We writers are so often told to write of the familiar, but what of imagination? Are our words not an opportunity for us to stretch our wings? An invitation not to speak of what is presented, but to speak of what is implied? Familiarity breeds an acceptance of idiosyncrasy, and the idiosyncrasy ceases to be observed. As strangers do we not see with foreign eyes?

I come here and I am swept backwards into my own imagination. I am unaware of the future, and thus am also unaware that I will be asked to convey my thoughts about what I am seeing and feeling. It is only later, much later, that such a request is made. I accept it gratefully, yet cautiously. How can you describe what you feel in so few words? How can you detail thirteen centuries of existence in thirteen paragraphs? You can but try to say something, though whatever you say will never be sufficient. You have to be here. You have to stand atop West Cliff and feel the wind, to stand on the pier and look up towards the Abbey, to see what Stoker saw, and thus appreciate that a place such as this has the power to invest everyone's imagination with a truly unique response.

And yet, is there something beyond this? Is there some presence here that possessed the power to fire that imagination? Is there something here that – even now – draws the gothic enclaves here for celebration?

Here there are legends too. Here they possess their own Baskerville Hound – the Barguest, the Padfoot, the Scriker, the Gytrash? What of this huge black beast, its eyes afire, the horrifying sound of its baying a warning to whosoever heard it that their life would shortly end?

What of the black-caped figure hurrying between the old Town Hall and The Black Bull Inn, a figure that possessed the power to walk unchecked through the body of a man?

What of the black-winged cormorant that circles and swoops and haunts the sky?

And the view from Spion Kop out towards East Cliff, such a view obscured by black waves of screeching bats. What of this?

Was Dracula here in his many incarnations long before Stoker arrived?

And the headless soldier at Baxtergate, standing silent as mother and daughter passed by, and hours later the news that a nearby Whitby family had lost their son in the Great War, his cause of death decapitation.

The Sacrament Piece; the Coffin Ring; the Abbess Hilda, a tale told by Sir Walter Scott, 'How, of a thousand snakes, each one, was changed into a coil of stone when the holy Hilda prayed.'

And yet again the phantom, even now walking the path between Prospect Hill and Ruswarp, the burden of its own gruesome head carried beneath its arm.

The unexplained sinking of the ship out near Black Nob, said ship charged with the duty of carrying back to London the Abbey bells by Henry VIII himself after the Dissolution. Despite the calm sea, the bright and fair sky, the people of Whitby came together and prayed that the bells would never leave. And the ship was swallowed by the ocean, and every sailor was drowned and was never recovered. It is said that on a quiet night, even so many centuries later, the sunken bells can still be heard to chime.

Is there some inherent darkness here, where lost souls walk these hills and cliffs, where they look out to sea, where they yearn for release?

Have the souls of history resided here forever, unable to leave, torn between the life they lived and some other life promised, and yet feeling so bound to this, their home, that departure became impossible?

Are not the streets and alleyways crowded with this multitude, this living, breathing memory of all that has taken place here?

Or is this imagination, the same imagination that was fired for so many others?

I walk further. I look back. The sea is dark like slate, like iron. The sun flickers from its surface like snaps of cold fire. The ships are motes of dust. The ocean supports these vessels without thought, and could swallow them without effort.

The wind carries you forward to the water's edge, and there you stand along the pier, your skin taut, your eyes brimming with tears of cold, and you hold the iron rail for fear of falling. The sea is deep and dark, and it has seen these shores through all the generations of Man, and still it does not leave.

I will leave, but I will remember this place. I will cast my mind back, I will stand right here once more, and feel these self-same thoughts.

I know I will return, and when I return will I find the same place, or something else? Will I find a new and unseen facet awaiting me?

There are those that belong, and have always belonged. There are those born here, and they will die here too, and never wanting for some other country, some other world, they are patient enough to watch as the sea brings the world to their feet. There is a unity here, where water meets earth, where the moon directs the tides, where a thousand years of stone becomes a thousand grains of sand.

And on clear days, when the ocean reflects the heavens, when the sea and sky are one and the horizon disappears, could this be the very end of the world itself? Could the ghosts I perceive be nothing but some internal spectre, as if the shadows of my own imagination merely serve to reflect some innate and inherent fear that belongs not here, but within?

Did I dream these things? Did I carry these thoughts with me, or were they here when I arrived?

Surely not, for the sea is clear now – an azure sheet, the sky like some bold sweep of colour from the artist's palette - cerulean and turquoise and sapphire. And the voices of children through these narrow streets, and the fellowship of friends and new acquaintances, and the warm hands of the high sun as the fog lifts and dissipates…and all is well here. Surely this is a town like any other? Surely there is nothing here but what I see in this bright and bracing summer's dawn?

And yet, as evening falls, as darkness once again approaches - if you still your thoughts, your mind, your heart - perhaps you can indeed hear the sunken bells, or the creaking of Demeter as she makes her approach to the shore, or the howling of the Barguest in the blackests of night.

Perhaps indeed there is some hidden history here, a history that serves to further enchant and intrigue, a history that merely brings a yet more beautiful facet to this place…

Whitby's East Pier silhouetted against the morning sun. (Rod Slater)

On Whitby Pier looking back towards the town. (Rod Slater)

The day fades out and the night begins to enclose Whitby Abbey. (Yorkshire Post Newspapers)

This Whitby...

This jet-black jewel of the eastern coast.

Rugged cliffs and a wheeling gull between Scarborough and Filey. (Rod Slater)

BLAKE MORRISON

Scarborough

Blake Morrison was born in a village near Skipton on the edge of the Yorkshire Dales. After working for the *Times Literary Supplement*, he went on to become literary editor of both the *Observer* and the *Independent on Sunday*. A Fellow of the Royal Society of Literature, Blake has written fiction, poetry, journalism, literary criticism and libretti, as well as adapting plays for the Halifax-based theatre company Northern Broadsides - among them *The Cracked Pot* and *The Man with Two Gaffers*. His best-known works are probably his poetry collection *The Ballad of the Yorkshire Ripper* and his two memoirs, *And When Did You Last See Your Father?* and *Things My Mother Never Told Me*. His latest novel *The Last Weekend* is published by Chatto & Windus. For further information visit www.blakemorrison.com

Blake's contribution is in narrative form. He tells the story of a teenage trip to Scarborough and marries his tale with some illuminating history of the resort. And if any readers can identify the ladies' lavatory he describes, we'd be keen to hear from you...

It was love above a public lavatory. The first time I'd fallen for someone. And in such a place! But if love could take root in the unloveliest of settings, it must be for real. As I told my friend Stephen afterwards, if God had appeared that night and said 'You have a choice, son: either the girl dies or your father does', the choice would have been easy. Sorry, dad, I know it's unfair. I met her only six hours ago, and a damp concrete floor above a public lavatory in Scarborough isn't the most romantic of venues. But what can I do?

*

'Do you fancy going to Scarborough?'

Scarborough. Why Scarborough, I thought? Scarborough was....east. The other compass points had prepositions to accompany them and clear associations too: down south (idleness), up north (hardship), out west (adventure). But what did east mean? Only exotic, and no one ever called Scarborough exotic. On childhood holidays we'd always gone west, to Morecambe, Southport, Anglesey, the Lleyn Peninsula. If Yorkshire had had a west coast I'm sure we'd have gone there too, but it was turn right out the front drive, never left. There'd just been the once, a trip to Redcar to visit an old colleague of my parents, after which we spent a night at Robin Hood's Bay. But Hull, Staithes, Bridlington, Filey, Whitby, Scarborough – all were unknown to me. And what I'd seen of the east I didn't much like. To me a coast meant inlets, coves, offshore islands, white breakers in an emerald ocean, not long straight strands and a dull brown sea.

So when Mikey, a friend from grammar school, cooked up a plan to go to Scarborough, I wasn't enthralled.

'Scarborough,' I said, 'what's the point?'

The point seemed to involve relations of Mikey who lived nearby, and pubs that weren't too strict about serving sixteen-year-olds, and hordes of available girls. My other two friends, Stephen and Brian, were keen.

'Why not Filey?' I said. 'There's a Butlins.'

'Butlins is for kids.'

'There'll be girls there.'

'Not as many as in Scarborough.'

'But there's nothing to do in Scarborough. It's posh.'

Poshness was the last thing I wanted. I was the doctors' son from the big house, desperate to be one of the people. Inverted snobbery, my mother called it. Nostalgie de la boue. Or nostalgie de Butlins.

'What you on about, Morri?' Mikey said. 'There's a funfair. And arcades. And a bowling alley. It's not Scarborough that's posh, it's you.'

My objections were rebounding on me. Any more and they'd be taking the piss.

'All right then.'

'Next week?'

It was agreed we split into pairs and hitch-hike, Mikey with Brian, me with Stephen.

'What should we take?'

'Sleeping bags. We might kip rough.'

'Not swimming trunks?'

'Get out. It's not a fucking beach holiday.'

*

Mikey might have been right about my own poshness. But I wasn't wrong about Scarborough's. Like Harrogate, it was a spa town and a preserve of the middle class. When mill-workers had their wakes week, they went to resorts that were cheap and cheerful, not ones famed for health-restoring waters.

I knew that much even at sixteen though I'd no idea how far Scarborough's origins as a spa town dated back - to the 1620s (just after Shakespeare's death), when a Mrs Farrow, 'a Gentlewoman of good Repute', noting the russet tincture and acid taste of the local water, 'thought it probable to have some medicinal quality, and thereupon did both try it her self, and perswaded others also that were sickly to drink of it…it became the usual Physick of the Inhabitants of Scarborough, and by degrees it came into use and reputation among those of the East-Riding near adjoining….At length it became well known to the Citizens of York, and the Gentry of the County, who do constantly frequent it, yea and to several Persons of Quality in the Nation…Nay I have met with several that have been at the Italian, French and Germane Spawes, who prefer this…before them all.' Thus reports a Dr Wittie, who goes on to list all the diseases of head, stomach, lungs and nerves which the spa at Scarborough is said to cure: apoplexy, epilepsy, catalepsy, vertigo, jaundice, asthma and leprosy, as well as 'Hypochondriack Melancholly and Windiness.'

My fear was that Scarborough would be exclusively populated by the geriatric well-to-do — that instead of cheap beer and easy girls, we'd find only wheelchairs and walking sticks. For me, the place was associated with illness and death. Though I wasn't a great reader in my early teens I did know about the Brontes' tragic lives, and how Anne, having spent holidays in Scarborough as a governess, returned there when she knew she was in danger of dying. 'The doctors say that change of air or removal to a better climate would hardly ever fail of success in consumptive cases if the remedy were taken in time,' she wrote before she went, 'but the reason why there are so many disappointments is that it is generally deferred till it is too late.' So it was with her. She arrived with Charlotte and their friend Ellen Nussey on a Friday morning. The following day, a trip to the baths left her exhausted. On the Sunday she sat in the window of her lodgings gazing out to sea. On the Monday she was so weak that Ellen had to carry her downstairs for breakfast. A doctor was summoned, who expressed wonder at 'her fixed tranquility of spirit and settled longing to be gone'. She died at two that afternoon.

It wasn't Scarborough that killed Anne, but the damp parsonage and unhealthy climate of the Pennines — the same sort of house and climate that I lived in. Still, the idea that a place on Yorkshire's east coast could cure anyone seemed ridiculous to me. Scarborough was a place to grow old and die in, not to have fun. Why had I agreed to go?

*

The hitch-hiking was slow. Two teenage boys with rucksacks - if I'd had a car, I'd not have picked us up, either. But eventually, umpteen rides later, we arrived, round seven in the evening. 'Where've you been?' Brian said, at the bowling alley where we'd arranged to meet, 'we've been waiting yonks'. Mikey, bored, had gone off in search of cheap lodgings. With the coffee bars closed and the discos not yet open, the bowling alley was the best place to find girls but the few we could see were all with boyfriends. I went to the counter, to buy Fantas and Cokes. 'You look like Paul McCartney,' a girl with bunches said. I doubted this was a compliment — John, not Paul, was the cool one — and anyway she looked about twelve.

We sat with our drinks cans, watching the bowlers pick up the shiny balls, hug them to their chest, take a few steps, bend, swing back, sweep forward and let go. Most of them were useless, except for one stylish bugger, with slicked back hair, bowling on his own. Jack Flash we called him; as he let the ball go, his right heel would flip up horizontally, like one of those indicators on an old Morris or Austin.

Mikey appeared, saying he'd found us a place to stay.

'Where?'

'On the front.'

'Must be pricey.'

'It's free.'

'Get out.'

Scarborough's own limestone promontory and historic castle form landmarks which are seen far out at sea. It is a town of elegant Georgian and Victorian buildings, spacious parks, sandy beaches and a lively harbour. (Yorkshire Post Newspapers)

**Two views of Scarborough circa 1960.
(Yorkshire Post Newspapers)**

'Scarborough is incomparable, both as a seaside resort and as a centre for exploring the Yorkshire coast and moors. Well has this delightful place been called the Queen of Watering Places, for it offers something for everyone. Pleasure and beauty are the keynotes, and the place has made the most of its natural charm.'

Yorkshire Revealed, G Douglas Bolton, 1955.

Scarborough Spa Bandstand and the Lunar Park ferris wheel.
Traditional seaside activities still draw good crowds. (Yorkshire Post Newspapers)

'In the nineteenth century Scarborough's development as a seaside resort continued apace but the resort concentrated on preserving its selectness and few concessions were made to the tastes of the masses. Evening dress was de rigeur on the Spa after sundown and entertainment was confined to an orchestra and one or two pierrot shows.'

Nowt so queer as folk, Derrick Boothroyd, 1976.

'It's above a Ladies bog.'

'What?'

'You heard. I ran into a bloke who slept there. He tipped me off.'

'Doesn't it stink?'

'No. You shin up a drainpipe and…'

Bang in front of us, in the alley next to Jack Flash, a group of girls had arrived and were lacing up their bowling shoes. About our age, by the look of it. Two blondes, one redhead, one brunette. Not bad-looking, either. In fact a couple of them were proper fit. It seemed too good to be true: four of them and four of us.

We watched for a while, then when Jack Flash wound up we paid for a round and took his lane. Boys being boys, we made a show of using the heaviest balls. The girls showed no sign of being impressed. But over the clatter of pins or (more often) the rumble of misplaced balls in the gutter, Mikey started chatting them up.

'Been bowling before?'

'Never,' the redhead said. 'Can't you tell?'

Her ball dwindled into the gutter halfway down.

'Keep your wrist straight. Like this, see.'

Mikey's ball veered left, clipping the outside pin. The girls giggled. But with her second ball the redhead took his advice. Her ball trickled down the middle, hitting the centre pin a fraction to the left.

'A ten, a ten!' she shouted, jumping up and down.

'A spare, you mean.'

'What's a spare?'

'If you'd done that with your first ball, you'd have a strike.'

'What's a strike?'

We explained about strikes and spares, and how the scoring system worked, then asked them their names. Fiona, Becky, Lavinia and Anne-Marie. Posh girls. All from the same boarding school in Surrey.

'So what are you doing in Scarborough?'

'Fiona's aunt lives not far away. We're staying with her.'

Fiona was the quiet one and seemed less friendly than the others – as if we'd gatecrashed her party.

'So doesn't your aunt mind you stopping out late?' Mikey said.

Fiona ignored him.

'It's only nine o'clock,' Becky said, 'The last bus isn't till eleven.'

I fancied Becky. She'd straight brown hair, a stripy jumper and flared jeans. If she thought us rough – boys from Skipton not Eton – she didn't show it.

'What you up to next?' we asked, as they swopped their bowling shoes for leather boots.

'We're going to the fair.'

'There isn't a fair,' Mikey said.

'Aunt Jacqueline said there was. A funfair anyway.'

'There's only arcades, and they're rubbish.'

I could have kicked Mikey. Didn't he want to stay with the girls? I was ready to follow them anywhere.

'Have a drink with us,' Mikey said, atoning. 'I know a nice pub.'

Fiona looked doubtful but the others were up for it.

Two hours in Scarborough and we'd struck lucky. No spares, either: four of them, four of us.

*

Are you going to Scarborough Fair
Parsley, sage, rosemary and thyme
Remember me to one who lives there
She once was a true love of mine

On the way to the pub, as if by instinct, we fell into pairs. Becky, alongside me, was humming the Simon and Garfunkel song. We all knew it, of course: it hadn't been out that long. But somehow I'd never associated it with Yorkshire. Simon and Garfunkel were American and I assumed there was Scarborough in the US (there is, in Maine – one of the first New England settlements) or that a fair so beguiling as the ballad made it sound must be imaginary.

I now know, thanks to Wikipedia, that in the late Middle Ages Scarborough (Yorks) did have a fair, one of the largest in Europe. It ran for 45 days each year and attracted traders from far and wide, until rival fairs drove it out of business - it finally folded in 1788. As for the song, it's said to derive (Wikipedia again) from an old Scottish ballad, 'The Elfin Knight', in which an elf threatens to abduct and rape a young woman unless she can perform an impossible task; cunningly, she pre-empts this by setting him a series of impossible tasks and thus saves her skin. But as a teenager I'd never really listened to the words, only the refrain, which was sad and elegiac and appealed to my adolescent self-pity.

'Do you like Simon and Garfunkel?' Becky asked.

'So-so. They're a bit too folky for me.'

The Richard III House stands opposite the harbour. Though it's claimed Richard III stayed here when he visited Scarborough, there's no evidence to verify this. (Rod Slater)

Scarborough Light House and Lunar Park against a brooding sky. (Yorkshire Post Newspapers)

'I love folk,' she said. 'Bob Dylan, Joan Baez, Donovan....' I was already regretting my so-so, and worried that Stephen, whose musical tastes were the same as Becky's, would overhear, interrupt and lure her away. Luckily Stephen, just behind us, was too preoccupied with Anne-Marie.

'Anyway,' she went on, 'it's a protest song.'

'Is it?'

What I'd picked up of the lyrics sounded fey to me. Cambric shirts and leather sickles – it was nonsense verse, Alice in Wonderland stuff.

'I never realised,' I said.

'No one does,' she said. 'Simon sings over Garfunkel and drowns his words. Or Garfunkel over Simon – I never know which. The words people hear are the hallucinogenic bits. They think it's a song about drugs.'

'Like *Lucy in the Sky with Diamonds*,' I said.

'Or a *Whiter Shade of Pale*. And maybe it is a bit druggy. But a girl at school told me the other words, the ones it's hard to hear. I think they're on the album cover. "Generals order their soldiers to kill...And to fight for a cause they've long ago forgotten". It's an anti-war song. They're talking about Vietnam.'

I didn't dispute it. I was too busy wondering what Becky knew about drugs and if she'd ever smoked pot.

Parsley, sage, rosemary, and cannabis.

Here I am in Scarborough, I thought. There's no fair but I have met a fair maid. And already I'm half in love.

*

Four pints of Tetleys, two Babychams, one Bacardi and Coke, one lager and lime: like us, the girls were happy to flout under-age drinking laws. At least three of them were: Fiona seemed more apprehensive. Or perhaps she was just unhappy with the way things were shaping up. On the walk and round the table the eight of us had paired off, and she'd been left with Mikey, who was trouble – a Heathcliff in the making. Still, a couple of drinks and Fiona seemed to relax. There was a lot of banter about how to say 'grass' and 'bath', which I didn't join in. I was conscious of Becky's arm next to mine. She had a sweet face, shining eyes, a gentle laugh. Her being from Surrey was part of the attraction too. There I was, despite myself, in thrall to poshness.

'Tell 'em where we're staying, Mikey,' Brian said.

Mikey said nothing at first. What would they think of us, if they knew? But Brian persisted, and once the girls joined in the coaxing Mikey gave in.

'Over some public bogs.'

'What?'

'Above a Ladies toilet. On the front.'

'We haven't slept there yet,' I said, as if that made it better.

'Yuk,' Becky said, but she laughed as she said it. Anne-Marie and Lavinia were laughing too. There were jokes about ghosts and chains.

'Isn't it damp?' Fiona said.

'Only when it rains,' Mikey said.

'And we've sleeping bags,' Stephen said, pointing to his rucksack. Brian and I had ours with us too. Only Mikey was without – he'd left his in situ, to claim the territory.

'The smell must be terrible.'

'Nah,' said Mikey. 'There's a concrete floor between you and the bogs. You shin up a drainpipe and…'

The talk turned to other things. Most of it passed me by. Three pints to the good, I was in love, and began to believe Becky must be too. Why else was she still sitting next to me?

Last orders were 10.30, a cue to leave for the bus station. But whether from inertia, inebriation, infatuation or incompetence, we were slow to get going. And by the time we got there, the bus had gone.

'Not to worry,' Mikey said, 'there's room at our place.'

The girls went into an anxious huddle round the phone box. There was talk of taxis or a B&B for the night, but they'd not much money on them, it was already gone 11 and everywhere was shut.

'You'll be safe with us,' Mikey said. 'Promise.'

Finally, Fiona entered the box and inserted her coins. We couldn't hear what she was saying but we could see her nodding her head. She seemed upset when she emerged, and none of us spoke for a while, in sympathy: we knew she had to perjure herself. Soon, though, we were giggling. Lying to adults was a necessary part of teenage life and essential for their own protection. Why expose Fiona's aunt to pointless fretting? The girls would be fine.

*

On the way to our lodgings, Becky and I picked up where we'd left off and talked about anti-war songs. I quoted some Wilfred Owen at her, the only poet I could quote – we were studying him for A-level. I'd begun to write a few poems myself and used a lot of alliteration and half-rhyme, just as he'd done in 'Miners'.

I thought of some who worked dark pits

Of war, and died

Digging the rock where Death reputes

Peace lies indeed.

Comforted years will sit soft-charred

Scarborough's fishing industry is still active, though only a shadow of its former self. The working harbour is home to a fish market including a shop and wooden stalls where fresh, locally-caught seafood can be purchased by the public. (Yorkshire Post Newspapers)

Scarborough harbour in the quiet of the early morning. (Rod Slater)

In rooms of amber;

The years will stretch their hands, well-cheered

By our lives' ember.

It was years later before I discovered that Owen wrote that poem while staying in Scarborough, at the Clifton Hotel in North Bay (which our walk must have taken us straight past). During the First World War, the hotel - then called the Clarence Gardens - had served as an Officers' Mess, and Owen, who undertook clerical work in his post as Mess Secretary, drafted some poems on the side. His room was a turret room – just like the one I stayed in when I returned to Scarborough, for the first time in decades, in 2008. What you see from the window is waves, roofs, seagulls, skies stretching to the horizon. But Owen's subject wasn't celestial but subterranean – war as a coal pit.

I wish I'd known about Owen and Scarborough when I was walking with Becky; it might have impressed her. But I knew very little in those days. And even now you wouldn't want me on your team in a pub quiz. Scarborough's most famous dramatist? That's easy: Alan Ayckbourn. But I didn't learn till recently that an earlier English playwright, Sheridan, wrote a play called *A Trip to Scarborough*. Nor did I know that another well-known twentieth-century poet had Scarborough connections: Edith Sitwell, who grew up in a house called Wood End. Perhaps in her case my ignorance can be forgiven, since Wood End was only one of several Sitwell homes (the family owned others in Derbyshire, Lincolnshire and London), and her contacts with the local community were minimal. It's not unusual for poets to be head-in-the-clouds but Sitwell ('the arch-nurse of empty phrases' as Julian Symons called her) was also nose-in-the-air – snobbish, rootless, a poseur. Who'd ever guess, reading her work, that she hailed from Yorkshire? Or think to include her – along with Marvell, the Brontes, Ted Hughes, Donald Davie, Tony Harrison and Simon Armitage – in the pantheon of Yorkshire poets?

*

Loveless: How do you like these lodgings, my dear? For my part, I am so pleased with them, I shall hardly remove whilst we stay here, if you are satisfied.
Amanda: I am satisfied with everything that pleases you, else I had not come to Scarborough at all.
Loveless: Oh, a little of the noise and folly of this place will sweeten the pleasures of our retreat…
[from Sheridan, 'A Trip to Scarborough', 1777]

'You shin up the drainpipe and…'

Here we were, in the dark and drizzle, round the left-hand side of the Ladies, listening to Mikey's instructions. Waves broke far off. None of us had a torch but there were streetlights. At the top of the drainpipe, ten feet above the ground, was a square opening, like a hatch. Half the excitement – and the girls were noisy with it

– was the climb.

'Keep your voices down. There could be a copper.'

Mikey led the way, squeezing through headfirst then turning to reach down and help the next climber.

'Come on, it's easy.'

We let the girls go first – with Fiona the fourth and most reluctant – then followed behind them. Inside was pitch black, until your eyes adjusted. There wasn't room to stand but you could sit up without banging your head. Where the floor was dry, away from the puddles at the far side, we unrolled our sleeping bags in a square, and sat on them – all eight of us - swigging from a whisky bottle that Mikey claimed to have nicked from the Co-op. For a while we spoke in whispers but once the whisky kicked in we grew less cautious, and soon we were singing songs. Becky, sitting next to me, had the best voice. Or so I thought. I was too far gone by then to be objective. I'd decided she was The One.

In theory we could have sat up all night. The pretence was that we would. There'd been no kissing, or none I could see or hear. But once the bottle was empty and the last cigarette smoked we began to lie down together, in pairs. And as it got colder, we wriggled into the sleeping bags - a tight squeeze for two people, with the zip done up, but, along with the jeans and jumpers we were wearing, useful protection against the cold. Becky's cheek was warm against mine. I stroked her hair and kissed her lips but that was all. I'd no idea how a posh girl would feel about having her breasts touched. And I didn't want to scare her away.

From the noises in the dark, it became clear that Mikey was playing it differently. 'No,' Fiona kept saying, 'No, get off, no, stop it, no.' She sounded upset, not merely playing-hard-to-get, but none of us said or did anything. Would an 'Are you all right?' from the girls or 'Leave it out, Mikey' from us have made a difference? In my head, as I replay the scene, her distress stretches through the night. But perhaps it was just a few minutes when we first lay down. In time, despite the cold and discomfort, we must have slept, or at any rate I did, because the next I knew was dim light seeping through the hatch and Becky slipping from my side. I grabbed her hand to stop her leaving but she pulled away.

'Fiona's crying,' she said, 'we have to go.'

Rejecting our help, the girls shinned down the drainpipe and were gone. I lay in the dark, nursing my loss.

'Fancy a walk?' Stephen said. We left Mikey and Brian snoring. Outside there were puddles and a drizzle of rain and sea-fret. It was still only six-thirty.

I told Stephen I was in love and that if God had appeared in the night and made me choose between letting Becky die or my dad, I'd have chosen my dad.

'That's daft,' he said, but then admitted he too felt lovelorn.

'They'll be back home having breakfast with Fiona's aunt by now.'

'Unless…When's the first bus go?'

'Shit. You're right. They might still be here.'

Formerly known as The Scarborough Museum, The Rotunda was completely redeveloped in 2008 with the aid of a generous grant from the Heritage Lottery Fund. It houses one of the foremost collections of Jurassic geology on the Yorkshire Coast. (Rod Slater)

Gardens on north side of The Grand Hotel. The lift to the beach can also be seen. (Rod Slater)

We ran all the way to the bus station and found them in the café, huddled round mugs of tea. They wouldn't look at us so we sat at a different table. When the bus came in and they got up, we followed. But they were already climbing aboard. 'Can we see you again?' we shouted after them, but they pretended not to hear. The doors shut and the bus pulled out of the station. We were ready to wave if they looked at us. But none of them did.

We went back to the toilets. I'd a copy of Kerouac's *On the Road* with me, and I lay reading it. I'd have done better to have a copy of Yeats. 'Love has built his mansion in the place of excrement,' he writes in one of his Crazy Jane poems, a line I'd have quoted at Becky if I'd known it.

*

'She'd not let me in her knickers,' Mikey said, later that day, as we sat eating fish and chips. 'She'd not even let me touch her tits.'

'Mine did,' said Brian, who seemed to have forgotten her name, 'but they were tiny. Like crab apples.'

Mikey laughed. Stephen and I said nothing. What we'd felt for Becky and Anne-Marie was pure, innocent, beautiful. We'd not demean it with laddish banter.

Next morning it was raining and we didn't venture out till gone midday. Mikey and Brian talked excitedly of cracking a particular fruit machine in the arcades; they could tell when it was due to pay out. Stephen and I left them to it while we wandered moodily along the front, talking about Becky and Anne-Marie. What did they look like? I wasn't sure any more. It was as if I'd imagined it all.

'I wish we knew where they were staying,' Stephen said.

'In a village, they said.'

'The bus was going to Whitby.'

'There can't be that many villages nearby.'

'And we know it's near the sea - Anne-Marie said they went swimming every day.'

'Shall we buy a map?'

We bought a map. And went to the bus station, to check the route of the Whitby bus. Only one village seemed to fit. Ravenscar. The next bus left in an hour, at half past three.

'Brian and Mikey won't want to come.'

'But we'd better tell them.'

We told. They were dismissive.

'Waste of fucking time.'

The route was slow and circuitous, and Ravenscar, when we reached it, looked bigger than shown on the map. Now we'd got there, the plan seemed stupid. We couldn't go knocking on doors and asking 'Are four girls staying here?' The beach was deserted. And there was no café or park or village green where they'd be likely to hang out. We trooped slowly back and forth past all the houses, hoping the girls would catch sight of us and come rushing out. By seven we'd given up and began to talk of getting back. Maybe an evening at the bowling alley would cure us of our stupid obsession.

Then we saw them. They were walking down the road, laughing and shouting. All four of them in a line, too wrapped up in themselves to notice us. All four, together with two boys.

The boys were tall and wore white cricket jumpers. One of them was holding hands with Becky, the other with Anne-Marie. When they saw us, the girls hesitated a little, but then kept going, straight past us. Nobody spoke a word.

It was Lavinia who turned back, the redhead who'd shared a sleeping bag with Brian, the one with crab apple breasts.

She was succinct about filling us in.

'Our boyfriends turned up. They're camping in a field. We didn't tell you about them because we thought we'd never see you again. We know it's not your fault about the other night. I liked Brian, we all liked you. Only…well, Fiona was very upset and we felt guilty and next morning was horrible. That's it really.…Sorry and all. Goodbye.'

Stephen and I wandered up the road, to where two tents had been pitched – a couple of boys were there, making a bollocks of lighting a fire. Further on was a pub and we sat there mooching in the dusk. The only bus back to Scarborough had already gone. Too miserable to care, we sat there till closing time. On the map, the back roads looked the shorter route. But the back roads were no good for hitch-hiking and we ended up walking all the way, reaching the Ladies sometime after two. Mikey and Brian were already asleep. However good a time they'd had, there were no girls with them. I lay awake wondering how long it would be before Becky tired of her boyfriend and realized her true love was me.

Next morning Stephen and I hitch-hiked home. A van driver took us to the outskirts of York, where the first car to come by was a Rolls Royce. We stuck out our thumbs for a laugh and the driver pulled up. He was wearing a uniform and cap, and gestured for us to get in. It turned out he was driving to Preston, to collect his boss, and would more or less pass our front door. We sprawled out on the leather seats, as if entitled to the luxury. After the low life above a Ladies, the high life in the back of a Rolls.

By next day, the Rolls, like the girls, seemed a dream.

*

I searched for the Ladies we'd slept above when I returned to Scarborough in 2008 but couldn't find them. Perhaps I looked in the wrong spot. Or they'd been pulled down. But I know I didn't imagine them. When I emailed Stephen the other day, he confirmed the details. 'They were set into the bank of the promenade, south of the bowling alley and on the sea front,' he says, though when he went back he couldn't find them either, and when he tells people about us sleeping there they think he must be making it up.

These old steps bridge Filey's beach area with Queen Street. (Rod Slater)

MARGARET DRABBLE

Filey

Award-winning novelist, biographer and critic Dame Margaret Drabble was born in Sheffield on 5 June 1939. She was educated at the Mount School in York, and read English at Newnham College, Cambridge. She became an actress and worked for the Royal Shakespeare Company at Stratford-upon-Avon before her first novel, *A Summer Birdcage*, the story of the relationship between two sisters, was published in 1963. Her other novels include *The Millstone, The Waterfall, The Ice-Age, The Radiant Way, The Peppered Moth* and *The Sea Lady*. Her latest book is the memoir, *The Pattern in the Carpet*, in which she looks at her own life, the history of games and the delights of puzzling. She is one of our finest writers.

She here recalls happy family holidays to Filey and finds continuous delight and inspiration from visiting this famous family resort.

Filey is for me the most numinous place on earth. It was once a little fishing village and is now a small seaside resort, a few miles south of Scarborough and north of Bridlington. The fishermen still go out to fish, but their haul today consists mainly of crabs and lobsters, not the codling and haddock and whiting we used to catch and eat for our high tea. My childhood memories of Filey, reinforced by rare visits in adult life, have a peculiar intensity, for this is a place that imprints itself deeply in the heart's affections. It survives, astonishingly, and its mood is much as it was when I first saw it. The sea comes and goes, the waves break against the great smooth blocks of the majestically curved sea wall, and the wide bay stretches from headland to headland. The children play on the sands and swim in the shallows, and the fishing boats bob on the deeper waters. The view is unchanging, the contours indelible. The little town has changed, but not as much as most towns of its size have done, and the seascape seems immortal. It is not immortal, of course- just along the coast the red clay cliffs crumble and buildings occasionally slide dramatically into the sea. But the sense is of continuity, of endurance. The modest spirit of Filey has resisted erosion and invasion.

Holidaymakers have been coming here since the end of the eighteenth century, and the *Gentlemen's Magazine* of 1805 noted that it was 'resorted to in the summer season by numerous parties from Scarborough and Bridlington. Its inviting scenery and the peculiar advantages it possesses for sea bathing would soon render it one of the first places of that description in the North of England where suitable buildings were erected for the reception of permanent visitors'. This was a cue for development, and speculators soon noted the tip, but Filey never aimed for or achieved the busy and more bustling atmosphere of its popular neighbours. Filey was refined, and restricted its appeal to the more discriminating guest. We Drabbles were very discriminating, and I was instructed at an early age in the doctrine of its and our superiority. (We were nobodies, aiming to be somebodies- the most fastidious holiday-makers of all.) We came here for our summer holidays for years, and were very pleased with ourselves for our choice. We went on an occasional outing to fast-living Scarborough, where I was particularly enthralled by the diving boards and chutes of the fancy turquoise-blue chlorinated swimming pool, but it was always with a sense of righteous satisfaction that we returned to our quiet bay, our salt water waves, and our little rented fishermen's cottage in Mitford Street.

I learned to swim at Filey, supported in the icy water by my noble father, turning blue as he stood cupping my chin with his hand while I practiced my breast stroke. In the 1940s and 50s bathing was considered a normal, a required activity, and indeed it was popular much earlier than that, as highly coloured bracing postcards and posters from the 1920s and 1930s show. The East Coast and Filey for the Family, as advertised by L.N.E.R., showed healthy, happy children clambering on rocks, fishing, swimming and playing beach ball. And Filey was an ideal place to learn to swim- a spacious sandy beach, gently sloping, in a safe and sheltered bay without dangerous currents or hidden rocks. It was not always very warm, and black and white photos of us taken with a Box Brownie show shivering and goose pimples rather than an L.N.E.R. Technicolor glow, but we didn't mind the cold. (Those rubber bathing caps were very unbecoming.) We went swimming in all weathers, even in the rain. Every year I swallowed so much brine that I was obliged to spend a day vomiting, but that also was part of the full Filey experience.

Sea bathing came into fashion in the late eighteenth and early nineteenth centuries, a vogue somewhat caustically charted by Jane Austen. It was a new fad of which she did not wholly approve, and in *Sanditon*, her last unfinished work written in 1817 when she was already ill, she gives a satirical account of the impulsive Mr Parker's excessive enthusiasm for the development of the new South Coast resort of her title. He assures doubters that it will never become one of 'your large, overgrown places, like Brighton, or Worthing, of Eastbourne.' It is, he affirms, a small village, 'precluded by its size from experiencing any of the evils of civilization' yet nevertheless ripe, in Mr Parker's speculative view, for canvas awnings, blue shoes and nankin boots, parasols, a library and a billiard room, bathing machines and milliners. New dwellings rejoicing in names such as Prospect House, Trafalgar House, and Bellevue Cottage were springing up, and a Terrace with a broad walk in front of it 'aspired to be the Mall of the place.' Sanditon was very much on the Filey scale, although Filey developed a couple of decades later than the Regency fashions that Austen describes. (For its remoteness from the evils of civilization, compare the *Filey Official Guide* of 1925 which boasts that 'Filey has made no figure in history, being cut off by its natural position from the main current of events...').

Austen disliked too much bustle, and had a pre-romantic, Augustan view of the sea. The sea was dangerous, as her sailor brother would have told her. We remember that when Louisa Musgrave went to Lyme Regis in *Persuasion*, she nearly killed herself by jumping off the Cobb. Austen did not share Mr Parker's desire to be rocked in bed by the grandeur of the storm, and thought it unwise to build on cliff tops for the sake of a sea view. She had a point, as the owners of various properties on the North East Coast, including the doomed Holbeck Hall, were in time to recognise.

Her successor, Charlotte Brontë, in contrast, had a high romantic view of the sea, coloured by Victorian sentiment and her own love of the wild Yorkshire landscape. To her, Filey proved a haven, a refuge, and a consolation. A gulf both of period and of temperament separates the two women, and marks the shift from Sense to Sensibility. The development of the little town of Filey is part of this historic evolution.

As a child, I was unaware of the Brontë connection with Filey, and learned of it only in adult life. This is slightly surprising to me now, as we were a Yorkshire-bred family of readers familiar with the Brontë novels, but maybe in August we were too busy with pony rides, ice creams, sand castles and bathing huts to explore what were essentially mournful literary associations. I have since made good this ignorance, both on the page and on foot, and discovered when and why Charlotte made her way to Filey, and what has happened to the house where she stayed. The story of Charlotte's tragic visit to Scarborough with her sister Anne and her friend Ellen Nussey is well known: Anne, gravely ill with pulmonary tuberculosis, had a longing to see Scarborough once more, a town she loved and had described lyrically in her novel *Agnes Grey* (1847), and on May 24, 1849, the three women set off, hoping against hope that the change of air and better climate might do her good. But only days later, on May 28, at the age of twenty nine, she died at Wood's lodgings on the Cliff ('one of the best situations in the place')where the Grand Hotel now stands. She was buried in Scarborough, at Charlotte's request. Charlotte's dream of buying seaside bonnets had turned to 'dreary mockery'.

Charlotte was now the only survivor of the four Brontë children. Immediately after Anne's death and burial, Charlotte and Ellen travelled south, and on June 4 she wrote to her publisher William Smith Williams, 'No letters will find me at Scarborough after the 7th. I do not know where my next address will be. I shall wander a week or two on the East Coast and only stop at quiet lonely places…'On June 13 she wrote again, 'Filey, where we have been for a week, is a small place with a wild rocky coast- its sea is very blue- its cliffs are very white- its sands very solitary- it suits Ellen and myself better than Scarbro' which is too gay…' Charlotte and Ellen lodged with a Mrs Smith at Cliff House in Belle Vue Street, one of the first houses to be built in what local historian Michael Fearon describes as 'New Filey'. It was built about 1824, and at that time would have had an uninterrupted prospect of the sea: today a row of buildings, which went up a few years later, blocks the view. Cliff House is no longer on the cliff, and it no longer has a Belle Vue, and you have to look at it twice to be sure you are in the right place. As its present owner June admits, 'it doesn't look like an old building'. It is square, three-storeys high, with first floor sitting room windows from which earlier guests could gaze at the sea. It is now the Brontë Vinery and Café, where you can sit and have a mug of hot tea on a cold wet day, with a jacket potato and Prawn Marie Rose for £4.50, or cod, chips and peas for £6.50, and admire the astonishing vine, covered in bunches of green grapes, that flourishes above your head and covers the roof of the terrace tea-room as though it were in Italy or Spain. Charlotte Brontë must have seen this vine, for it is said to be hundreds of years old, and therefore would pre-date Cliff House. It seems to grow straight out of the pavement. It looks as though it could be plastic. It looks too good to be true. June (who used to be the railway crossing keeper at Muston Crossing) says that guests can't resist touching the grapes to see if they are real, which is not good for their bloom. How did I miss this phenomenon when I was a child? I feel sure Charlotte would have found it as exotic and unlikely as I now do. Or were vines more widely distributed a century or two ago?

Maybe it grew overnight, like something out of Jack and the Beanstalk.

The tea-room has cosy pink lamp shades and receives added colour from two rotating transparent plastic barrels, filled with a shocking pink and an electric turquoise-blue substance, which goes round and round as though it were in a very small Hadron collider. The young man serving at the counter tells me it is called Sludge. This is a new one to me. I sit and watch it, mesmerised, as I listen to Yorkshire Coast Radio playing gently and pleasantly and very politely. Even the commercial radio station is genteel here. And as I sit, I remember the treats of yesteryear- the ice creams on the beach, the decisions between cones and wafers,

The Brontë Vinery Cafe and vine. (Rod Slater)

A line of cobles wait for their next fishing adventure. (Rod Slater)

the occasional disappointment of candyfloss. I remember the cakes from Sterchi's, the historic confectioners just along the road in Murray Street, established by a Swiss chocolatier in 1919 and, amazingly, still going strong. (We pronounced it Sturchy, to rhyme with Churchy.) And I remember the first ice cream soda I ever encountered, in 1948, in a tiny café in a tiny side street somewhere near here. I didn't know what an icc cream soda was, but our minder, a very young woman called Patience (who considered Filey a bit too genteel for her) knew all about such things, and ordered them for us. As I recall, this treat consisted of some bright red fizzy pop in a tall fluted glass, topped with a ball of melting vanilla ice cream, a combination which you could attack either with a long spoon or with a straw. It was outlandish, sensational, and clearly wicked. I think I thought it was delicious, but at the same time slightly disgusting.

History does not record what treats were on offer to Charlotte Brontë and Ellen Nussey, but Charlotte clearly found Filey congenial, for she returned there alone in May 1852, staying again in Cliff House for a month, where she enjoyed walking on the beach, bathed once in the sea when the bitterly cold weather improved, and became 'almost as sunburnt and weather-beaten as a fisherman or a bathing-woman with being out in the open air'. On June 2, she wrote to her father: 'On the whole I get on very well here, but I have not bathed yet as I am told it is much too cold and too early in the season. The sea is very grand. Yesterday it was a somewhat unusually high tide, and I stood for about an hour on the cliffs yesterday afternoon watching the tumbling in of great tawny turbid waves, that made the whole shore white with foam and filled the air with a sound hollower and deeper than thunder. There are so very few visitors at Filey yet that I and a few sea-birds and fishing-boats often have the whole expanse of sea, shore, and cliff to ourselves. When the tide is out the sands are wide, long and smooth, and very pleasant to walk on. When the high tides are in, not a vestige of sand remains.'

She did not think so well of the church (possibly Speeton church on the cliffs, but more probably St Oswald's) and told her father, 'There is a well-meaning but utterly inactive clergyman at Filey, and Methodists flourish.' Pevsner thinks better of St Oswald's- 'easily the finest church in the NE Corner of the East Riding'- and he and other architectural historians have agreed that the Crescent is one of the best in Britain. Bronte, referring to the growing Crescent, noted in a letter to Ellen Nussey (6 June, 1852) that 'more lodging houses, some of them very handsome, have been built' since their last visit. Today, viewed from afar, the curve of the white classical columned buildings- hotels, apartments, and now retirement homes- forms a distinguished and harmonious whole. The Crescent Gardens, with their bandstand, offer a fine view over the bay, and I well remember watching the dashing Cossack Riders there. My father hoped they were real Cossacks, and maybe they were. Once every summer, I think for my sister's August birthday, we would have a celebratory tea in one of the big hotels, with cakes and silver cake forks. The road up from the beach is still cobbled, and the houses on the beach front have changed little. Ackworth House, one of the grandest of these, built as the Spa Saloon in the 1860s in the French Renaissance style, has been newly decorated and is now a residential home for the elderly. The views from the upper windows must be splendid.

The Cossack Riders were rare and exotic visitors, but we also went to one or two live revues with singing and dancing and incomprehensible jokes, and to regular viewings at the Brigg Cinema where the programme changed twice weekly. We never saw the famous Royal Filey Pierrots, who flourished before our time and had once played to the Battenberg family. Live entertainment was controlled, by public opinion if not by the Council. The 1925 *Official Guide* quotes approvingly a 'famous journalist' (unnamed) who wrote that,

'No nigger has yet desecrated Filey sands, there are no stalls, no palmists, no itinerant musicians. Cheap trippers never come here, and they are not wanted. If they did come they would feel themselves lost. Scarborough to the left and Bridlington to the right cater for the tripper. Filey views him with profound disdain.' ('Nigger' here presumably means 'nigger minstrel', which makes this boast slightly less offensive than it appears at first sight.) I do not remember any Punch and Judy shows. Amusements in Filey, like its architecture, were refined. It has no pier, no harbour, no vulgar promenade. But it does have Amusement Arcades and Crazy Golf, as it did in my day. We used to spend hours spending pennies in the Arcade, making little silver balls whiz round into holes or having our fortunes printed or trying to capture prizes with the grasping hands of little cranes. You can still shelter from the rain and waste your coppers in the Arcades.

The Crescent is grand, but the smaller, humbler streets and alleys of Filey give as much delight to the visitor, as do the little pathways and stairways that wind their way up and down the cliff and the cobbled Ravine at the north end of the town. Many of the little houses have pretty stained glass fanlights showing art nouveau flowers and nautical motifs- fishes, seabirds, little yachts, lifebuoys and the characteristic fishing cobles of the Coble Landing. The bay windows facing directly onto the streets also display enterprising assemblies of model boats, statuettes, pot plants, needlework and bric-a-brac. The details you can glimpse in the most architecturally ordinary dwellings are charming. Some of the original fishermen's cottages have unfortunately and controversially been demolished, but Filey Musem, with its date of 1696, retains the spirit and gives an impression of Old Filey. It overflows with historic artefacts, old photographs, postcards (including a surprising one of a black baby hatching out of an eggshell) and other memorabilia. 'There just isn't room to put everything', sighs one of the volunteer guides.

The town is pleasant, but the sea, the sands and Filey Brigg are more than pleasant. They are sublime. One of the best seaside walks in Britain must be the walk from the Coble Landing, past the Lifeboat House, past the bathing huts, past the little café on the cliff, and along the beach to the Brigg. The Brigg is a unique geological phenomenon, a natural pier or jetty, a promontory of rocks and boulders that stretches out to sea at the north end of the bay. There is an excellent account of its formation, through prehistoric times, in the Museum. Charlotte Bronte (who called it 'Filey Bridge') described it in a letter to her father as 'a black desolate reef' and later evoked a similar scene in Shirley (ch. 32); 'A reef of rocks, black and rough, stretches far into the sea; all along, and among, and above these crags, dash and flash, sweep and leap, swells, wreaths, drifts of snowy spray.' This is not a landscape Jane Austen would have been inclined to admire.

Century after century, the waves dash against the Brigg, and wash over it, and with every tide the rock pools fill and empty, ebb and flow, refreshing themselves perpetually as the waters rise and fall. The Romans knew the Brigg, and the emperor Constantine is said to have bathed in one of the caves, though that seems an unlikely story. Today it remains a paradise for children with fishing nets and buckets, for men with fishing rods. A 1920s postcard shows an elegantly dressed young lady in pink precariously perched on the edge of a rock with a rod and line, dangling her high heels over the foam, but in fact I've never seen a woman fishing there. It's always men.

The pools are home to an immense variety of marine life and are, in themselves, of extraordinary beauty. One pool I particularly love, a shallow pool with a pale shining silvery pink floor, on which limpets and other shells are arranged by nature with the greatest artistry, along with sea anemones and the pale green fronds and darker ribbons of reddish seaweeds. It is like a painting, an embroidery, an exemplary illustration

The Crescent's magnificent facade. (Rod Slater)

Ackworth House – former spa saloon. (Rod Slater)

'Years ago Filey obtained a reputation for being quiet, and the sense conveyed by those who disliked the place was that of dullness and primness. This fortunate chance has protected the little town from the vulgarising influences of the unlettered hordes let loose upon the coast in summertime, and we find a sea-front without the flimsy and meretricious buildings of the popular resorts.'

Yorkshire, Gordon Home, 1908.

These circa 1950 images all show working cobles and the effort that was required to launch them.
(Yorkshire Post Newspapers)

Fresh crabs brought ashore circa 1950. (David Joy Collection)

The south side of Filey Brigg, a shelving mass of limestone rock which runs far out into the sea. (Rod Slater)

The Jenkinson family were and still are a famed fishing family in Filey. The fare advertised here is still avidly bought and consumed by modern day visitors. (David Joy Collection)

FRANK JENKINSON,
(FISHERMAN)
FRESH
-BOILED - CRABS - MUSSELS -
SHRIMPS - WINKLES - COCKLES.

SHELLFISH

DRESSED CRABS
FRESH DAILY
COCKLES   6ᵈ PLATE
WINKLES   6ᵈ
MUSSELS   6ᵈ
WILKLES   6ᵈ
SHRIMPS

• COCKELS. 6ᵈ PLATE
• SHRIMPS. 6ᵈ Bag
• WINKLES. 6ᵈ Bag
• MUSSELS. 6ᵈ Plate
• CRABS FRESH DAILY

of the marvels of the sea shore. In the deeper pools, crabs scuttle, shrimps dart and small fish hide in the secret fissures and crevices. I have never seen a lobster on the Brigg, except on one occasion when I met some fishermen who had just caught one. They showed him off, a large dark blue mottled creature with great claws. And once, on the steep rocky northern side, I thought I saw a conger eel- a vast snake of a fish, ten feet long, swaying in the tide in a deep pool on a ledge. One can imagine all kinds of sea monsters lurking just out of sight. At the point of the Brigg, seabirds cluster. A colony of cormorants perches, hunched, sinister, prehistoric, and gulls screech and swirl. The cormorants look as though they have been there since the Jurassic, long before Constantine came this way.

The Brigg is dangerous at high tide, and you are warned to time your walk with care in order not to get cut off. The plaque in the Life Boat House lists recent rescues and indeed the recovery of a dead body. This drama, of course, adds to the excitement of the excursion. But it is slightly easier of access than it was, because a rough concrete path now leads along most of its spine, making it easier to negotiate. There are patches where the path has been washed away and you have to climb and clamber, so it is still quite challenging. The concrete is unsightly. It is not an improvement.

It must also be admitted that some of the pools, despite the constant renewal of the tides, are not as crystalline as they were when I was a child. A slight scum infects some of them, a discolouration of algae, hinting at too many visitors or a wider ecological problem. But the waves wash away the litter, and on the whole, the Brigg has survived well. It still features in my dreams, an archetype of oceanic eternity. These dreams are more Jungian than Freudian, and Wordsworth would have recognised their pattern. He knew about the children playing upon the immortal shore.

My formative visits to Filey have made their way into my fiction, from the very beginning to the end of my career. When I was at university I wrote a short story about a rock pool which mingled memories of the Brigg with an expedition to Elba when I was seventeen: it's about bravado, pollution and desecration, and could be interpreted as foreshadowing our current ecological anxieties, though that's not what I thought it was about at the time. Granta declined to publish it, which discouraged me from writing fiction for a year or two, but eventually it appeared in a magazine, and will I trust find a permanent home in a collection of my stories due out in 2011. And my most recent novel, *The Sea Lady*, is full of seaside holiday recollections, transposed from Filey to a fictitious village called Finsterness which is located somewhere further up the coast, near Berwick. Filey and its imagery have been a continuing inspiration, a constant point of reference.

The beach at Withernsea. (Yorkshire Post Newspapers)

'whatever we lose (like a you or a me) it's always ourselves we find in the sea'

ee cummings.

ROY HATTERSLEY

Hornsea and Withernsea

Roy Hattersley is a British Labour politician, a renowned author and journalist. He is a regular contributor in the national press and has written many books including memoirs, biographies, novels and several social histories. His latest books are *Borrowed Time: The Story of Britain Between the Wars*; *David Lloyd George: The Great Outsider*; **and** *In Search of England*, **a passionate and affectionate exploration of the English countryside and character.**

He here presents a loving tribute to old-fashioned summer holidays and takes us on a journey to two of his favourite east coast resorts.

In the years before two weeks on the Costa Brava was a holiday aspiration within the reach of working families, the holiday resorts of the East Riding – known collectively in pre-war Yorkshire as "the sea-side" – all knew their place in the hierarchy of summer esteem. Scarborough – with two bays and as many big hotels – claimed top place. Filey came a good second, tying with Whitby, which had less refinement but more charm. In bottom place, Bridlington, the wholly justified reputation for being usually cheap and invariably cheerful was enough to keep its landladies content. But Hornsea and Withernsea did not figure in the social league table. Hardly heard-of outside the county and mostly patronised by Hull, they kept themselves to themselves in proper Yorkshire fashion and got on with their own business. They still do.

Hornsea does not even feature on the map which decorates the introductory page of "Explore Yorkshire", the National Trust's guide to "great days out". Admittedly it boasts neither stately home nor ruined priory. But neither do Driffield and Malton and their existence is acknowledged in the brochure. I doubt if the people of Hornsea either know or care about their exclusion. Part of the slightly dilapidated charm of the coastline between Bridlington and Spurn Point is its detachment from the modern idea of a holiday. Its two principal "resorts" – if such an exotic word is appropriate – are certainly neither luxurious nor loud. On a glorious summer's day, their beaches were virtually deserted – not, I regret in protest against the interdict on dogs. The explanation, repeated all the way down the coast was, "Wait until the school holidays". Hornsea and Withernsea are for families and all the better for it.

Few families choose their holiday destinations because of the geological merits or agricultural potential of the area in which they are located. But the Holderness Plain, the hinterland of the East Riding coast, does merit a moment's consideration. A great glacier once passed that way, leaving behind sand and gravel flat-lands which turn into the East Yorkshire Wolds – open, undulating and, since it has few trees, exposed. The soil is so fertile that what used to be called the Ministry of Food and Fisheries classified it as A1 class farming land. The fields of waving wheat exude an air of agricultural well-being. Sadly, between the holiday towns, the potentially prosperous East Yorkshire is disappearing into the sea.

This view of Hornsea was taken circa 1950. (Yorkshire Post Newspapers)

Hornsea and Withernsea have chosen to ignore the lesson taught to his subjects by the much maligned and misunderstood King Canute and attempt to hold back the tide. In Hornsea the sea-wall is a concrete continuation of the sand dunes which might have been constructed in Normandy to frustrate the D-Day landings. In Withernsea it is embellished with twin towers (improbably modelled on Conway Castle) which confirm that man is as destructive as nature. They were built as the ceremonial entrance to the wooden pier, one thousand and two hundred feet long. So many ships collided with it – breaking off a yard or two in one decade and a few feet in the next – that the town council decided to demolish the stump which remained and declared the towers a civic monument in their own right.

Between Hornsea and Withernsea the sea is still eroding the land away. The villages along the B1242 –which connects the two towns – all stand back from the sea. By far the most historically distinguished is Aldbrough, the site of Isorium Brigantum and the Roman fortress that guarded the bridge by which Dene Street crossed the river Ure on what Richard Branson would call "the east coast route" to the north. The Normans moved the crossing west to Boroughbridge and, eight hundred years later, thanks to the great Reform Act, Aldbrough lost its two Members of Parliament. But the village remains symbolic of the East Yorkshire coast, past as well as present.

The George and Dragon in Aldbrough is a mile and a half from the beach – half a mile closer than it was when I used to visit it, fifty years ago. At its beginning, the road to the shore is depressingly urban – tar, footpath and yellow line. But at its end – still more suitable to a suburb than the sand hills through which it runs - it becomes a dramatic demonstration of the destruction wrought by time and tide. A concrete barrier – substantial enough to hold back a tank – prevents further progress. And on the other side there is only space. Travellers daring enough to lean over and peer down, discover a sheer cliff of the sort peculiar to Yorkshire's east coast – not limestone or granite but vulnerable dark brown soil. The general impression – perhaps the result of vertigo – is that a slice has been cut out of a giant chocolate cake.

It seems unlikely that residents of the Aldbrough Caravan Park would venture down to the seashore even if the road which once led to surf and sand did not end in mid-air. Two notices on the barrier describe the dangers down below. The first warns, "Unexploded ordnance on the beach. IT MAY KILL YOU." The second – presumably intended for visitors who are not easily intimidated – adds, "Do not approach or touch any military or unidentified object." Down the coast at Withernsea, the town council's advice to prospective bathers is equally stark. "PLAY SAFE! THE SEA IS NOT A SWIMMING POOL. Life guards do not protect this beach." The injunctions go on and on. "Do not take airbeds or inflatable toys into the sea unless supervised by an adult. At no time must they be taken into the sea when red flag is flying. BEWARE OF OFFSHORE WINDS." Then, after pictures of objects to be avoided at all cost, it all starts again. "IN THE SUN slip on a t-shirt, slap on a hat, slop on some sun-cream". The Yorkshire genius for understatement seems to have deserted the local safety, health and welfare officials.

After reading the stern injunction I was surprised to see half a dozen children, regardless of their doom, splashing about in a little pool left in the sand when the tide went out. Perhaps the children were determined to make the best of the sand before it disappeared. According to one prophet of local doom, in a bad year at Withernsea a full ten feet of beach is washed away. A Victorian antiquarian, called Shepherd, mapped out "The Lost Towns of The Yorkshire Coast" and located most of them in the deep water beyond the sand and pebble beach. On the Withernsea sea-wall a plaque records that "a mile off shore once stood the Church of

Hornsea from the air. (Yorkshire Post Newspapers)

The sea gets closer and closer to this caravan park. Along the Holderness coast the North Sea nibbles away at the land at around two metres a year – which equates to about two million tonnes of eroded material. (Yorkshire Post Newspapers)

St Mary the Virgin", "lost ever since the mid fifteenth century."

On a cloudless afternoon with the waves lapping gently against the lines of breakwaters that divide the East Coast beaches into regular fifty yard segments, it is difficult to believe that the sea offers any sort of threat. In both Hornsea and Withernsea, local residents fish with a tranquillity that borders on the complacent and certainly avoids all unnecessary exertion. Their tall fishing rods are leant against steel tripods which they have secured in the sand against a sudden gust of wind and their lines stretch so far out into the steel-grey water that the float is invisible to the naked eye. That does not matter. The fishermen do not watch anxiously for signs of a catch. They doze in plastic chairs, surrounded by vacuum flasks, baskets of provisions and cautionary umbrellas. When they move at all it is to reach out to pour a cup or to adjust a portable radio. Unlike many fishermen, they are willing to have their concentration disturbed by conversation. Occasionally they catch cod. But a more realistic expectation is "school bass" – young fish which swim in clusters and are thought to find lug worm irresistible. Digging the bait out of the sand must have been the fisherman's most energetic activity. At four o'clock one angler announced, "Here since half past eleven and haven't caught a thing." It was a statement of fact, not a complaint. He was happy just to be there.

It is not only contented fishermen that Hornsea and Withernsea have in common. Both towns have been buffeted by more than the North Sea. They have been overtaken by time and what passes for progress. It is wholly appropriate that one of the few remaining rows of Hornsea's boarding houses – which the locals now call "bed and breakfasts" - should be in Victoria Terrace. It runs behind the slightly forlorn Marine Hotel, which has clearly seen better days. The elderly men and women, who were playing bowls on the green in front of the Floral Hall, represent the traditional attraction of such places. But modern holidaymakers want something which is brighter and more brash. Hornsea exudes the impression that it is unable –or perhaps, to its credit, unwilling – to provide it. No music blares on its promenade.

Most of the twenty-first century visitors who stay for a week are accommodated in great estates of shining white mobile homes that never move from their cliff-top resting places. Some of them are garnished with pot plants and window boxes which suggest that they are holiday homes which are owned and rented by East Riding devotees who spent regular summer weekends on the Yorkshire coast, hoping for sunshine and sometimes finding it. If fourth millennium archaeologists sift through what the sea has left behind, they will probably conclude that the twenty-first century inhabitants enjoyed a restricted diet. In Hornsea, the fish and chip shops come not singly but in battalions. Sea Front Chips, Admiral Guest House Fish and Chips, Sullivan Fish and Chips, JB Fish and Chips – you can take your pick on the Hornsea sea front. The brochure – by which Withernsea, to the south, advertises its charms to the world – includes a profusion of fish and chip shops in its list of special attractions.

There was a moment in Hornsea's history when it became famous for its pottery – so famous that the uninitiated – like me – believed that clay had been thrown and then baked in the town's kilns since medieval times. In fact the Hornsea pottery was established in 1949 by local men who relied on local money to support their eclectic tastes. Some of their best work is on display in the Hornsea Museum in Newbiggin, the main street of the town, alongside tableaux of the town's past. The collection illustrates the pottery's two distinctive styles - crockery of severe design, glazed in white and plain primary colours and what are known in the trade as "posy vases" and "character jugs". The vases were decorated with embossed ceramic flowers –usually roses and violets – and the "characters", which or whom adorned the jugs, were animals. Rabbits and squirrels predominated. After several incipient bankruptcies and matching rescue operations, the company collapsed in 2000. Its products are still collectors' items. It says much for the discernment of the British public that the austere crockery is valued far more highly than the representation of cuddly animals.

Hornsea now claims that it is a good place to find a bargain. Perhaps it always was. Its long beaches made it easy for smugglers to bring their brandy and tobacco ashore without troubling the excise men and, according to local legend, they avoided discovery and arrest by hiding their contraband in the crypt of the parish church. Perhaps it is in tribute to their memory that the town's "shopping village" is called "Hornsea Freeport". Village it might just be. The shops stand in sylvan surroundings. But "Freeport" is a term more appropriate to a Danzig after the Treaty of Versailles than to a collection of retailers – many famous names among them – who certainly add VAT to the price of their goods. The "freeport" features large in Hornsea publicity. So does the beginning (or, if you are arriving in the town, rather than leaving it, the end) of the Trans-Pennine Trail - the spectacular track for hikers and cyclists that leads to Southport in the far West and joins sea to shining sea. But neither is Hornsea's main attraction. That, without the slightest doubt, is Hornsea Mere - a lake (left behind when a glacier slid by 10 million years ago) which is fed by East Riding fresh water streams and drains into the salty sea.

The guidebooks claim that Hornsea Mere – two miles long and three quarters of a mile wide – is the largest natural lake in Yorkshire. Perhaps when I was last in North Yorkshire, the altitude and the beauty of Wearnside, Ingleborough and Pennygent, made me overestimate the size of Malham Tarn – what heaven must look like if it is on high ground, its sky is cloudless and its air is clear. Or perhaps the guidebooks are wrong. They are certainly fallible. One says that Hornsea Mere is eight feet deep. Another puts the depth at twelve. Its dimensions are far less important than its inhabitants – both flora and fauna. The flora – sedge and reeds – give the mere an air of medieval mystery. Forget the doleful influence of La Belle Dame Sans Mercy. The sedge had withered from her lake and, in consequence, no birds sang. Hornsea Mere echoes to the sound of a dozen different species. And the northern bank belongs not to Keats palely loitering Knight at Arms, but to King Arthur. It is easy to imagine Excalibur looping over the reeds - after Sir Bedivere had, at last, obeyed his order - and the mystic hand rising out of the still water to catch the sword before returning it to eternity.

In the real world, Hornsea Mere is a nature reserve and RSPB bird sanctuary. Not all of its inhabitants are easily identified. The layman is unable to distinguish between dance-flies, crane-flies and the fearsome sounding snail-killing-flies. Indeed he might confuse any one of them with a wainscot moth. Nor does the thoughtfully provided explanatory poster provide much help. But it is well worth close study. Although it ignores the starlings which abound, it offers clear pictures of the gadwells, goldeneyes, reed warblers and tufted ducks which make the mere their home for half the year and the warblers, water rails, great crested grebes (which I had always believed to be heraldic or allegorical) and the little (a breed not a size) gulls which are resident for all the year. But the most impressive breed of bird is not mentioned in any of the educational literature. That, I suspect, is because it is common – not "common" in the East Yorkshire social sense but "common", meaning numerous, as ornithologists use the word.

 The star performers of Hornsea Mere are Canada geese and there are hundreds and possibly thousands of them on its eastern bank. Every one of them looks, indeed is, identical to the rest of the flock – same size, same marking and same air of self assurance. They all make the same urgent noise. And, most important of all, they are all tame. Indeed they behave as if they have been trained. They operate in what seems to be

Beach-casting on the Holderness shore between Skipsea and Hornsea. Sea-angling is a perennially popular activity. (Yorkshire Post Newspapers)

This crenellated folly is probably the most striking characteristic of Withernsea seafront. It was at one time the entrance to the original Withernsea Pier. The pier itself has long gone, but these impressive towers - nicknamed 'The Sandcastle' – remain. (Rod Slater)

Examples of Hornsea Pottery. In its heyday its tableware was sold right around the world. The pottery factory closed in 2000. (Yorkshire Post Newspapers)

carefully selected cadres. Some follow visitors to the mere with the single-minded devotion that the rats of Hamlyn displayed towards the Pied Piper. Others perform complicated aerial manoeuvres – swooping and climbing in what looks like choreographed unison. They are, of course, alien to the East Riding – immigrants who have made life more difficult for the decent locals. But the indigenous species mingle tolerantly with the interlopers - sharing, without visible antagonism, crusts dropped by careless tourists and the worms and grubs which inhabit the sand. A couple of spotless swans arched their necks in what might have been resentment. But apart from that spectacular exception, the culturally diverse birds of Hornsea Mere showed every sign of being a happy family.

Outside school holidays, Withernsea – like Hornsea – seems to go to sleep. At mid-afternoon on the day of my visit, all the cafes were locked and barred and only one tea-and-sandwich-take-away was open for business. Fortunately it was in the shadow of the town's unique attraction – the Withernsea Lighthouse and Kay Kendall Memorial Museum. The title needs some explanation. The Kay Kendall Museum is housed, as is a lighthouse museum, within the real Withernsea Lighthouse. Its light went out for the last time in 1976.

But, illuminated or not, the whiter-than-white lighthouse is itself a wonder. It towers, one hundred and twenty seven feet high, over Hull Street in the middle of the town. One guidebook says that it was built among sand-dunes. But that suggests that the sea is retreating. The lighthouse caretaker offers a more convincing explanation for its strange location. Had it been built - like an ordinary lighthouse - close to the sea, its foundations would have been washed away years ago.

An inland lighthouse – unlike those built at the edge of rocky promontories or on solitary pillars of stone in the sea – can accommodate its keeper in what approximates to a normal suburban house, rather than leave him to bed down in the lamp-house. The Kendal family were the lighthouse keeper's neighbour. That, and her sister's initiative, is why part of the lighthouse is dedicated to her memory. The centrepiece of the memorial is a wax effigy of Miss Kendal herself, reclining elegantly on a chaise longue with a cardboard cut-out of Rex Harrison, her husband when she died, hovering supportively behind her. The walls of the room which celebrates Hornsea's most famous daughter are covered in posters for the films in which she starred – *Genevieve* and *Les Girls*, a confusing title which, as a boy, I assumed related to its eponymous hero – and glamorous photographs of the star herself. Sometime during her all too brief career, the bridge of her nose – which could easily have launched a thousand ships – changed from convex to concave. The museum does not tell us how often, if at all, Miss Kendall returned to Withernsea during her glory years. If she did, how – I wonder – did her old friends react to the new and improved version.

The rest of the lighthouse pays homage to those in peril on the deep and the men on whom they rely at times of mortal danger. The most evocative exhibit is a collection of name boards from long beached Spurn Point lifeboats – all of them referring in some way to Bradford, which traditionally raised the money for renewal and repair. It is still possible to climb the one hundred and forty-four steps which make up the circular staircase that winds up the wall from ground floor to lamp room. Not all visitors are so inclined. School students, the caretaker assured me, particularly enjoy ascending to the heights. I suspect that they do not recognise the importance of what looks like metal junk lying in the yard. The rusting steel is a relic of the Second World War and includes the air-raid siren that once howled its warning from the roof of the town hall. Its baleful sound was a regular feature of Withernsea life. The lighthouse – tall and white against the sky – was used by German bombers as a signpost to guide their daylight raids on Hull.

One exhibit tells the story of what happened to Withernsea after the war. It is an advertisement for "Rail Excursions to Dancing at the Royal Pavilion" designed to attract the young Hull social set. In 1964, Doctor Beeching closed the stretch of track which began life in the nineteenth century as the Hull and Holderness Railway and severed one of the connections which made for Withernsea in summer, Hull's sea-side suburb. The bond has not been entirely broken. The accents and intonations are identical. Questions end with emphasis on the final misplaced conjunction. "What did you do that for?" And there is still good reason for Hullensian sunbathing enthusiasts to make a day trip north. Withernsea is their nearest "Blue Flag Beach", guaranteed for clean sand, unpolluted water and safety. The forbidding notice by the twin towers turns out to be a tourist attraction.

But then, both Withernsea and Hornsea are full of surprises. Perhaps the greatest – and certainly the most important – is the demonstration that the old-fashioned summer holiday has not quite passed into history. The two towns have changed with the years. But faint echoes of a more innocent past remain. They may soon be submerged in a deluge of redevelopment. Enjoy them while you can.

'So dawn goes down today, Nothing gold can stay.'
Robert Frost.

IAN MCMILLAN

East Coast Memories:
A Spurn Meditation

Born in Barnsley in 1956, Ian McMillan is a poet, broadcaster and comedian. He contributes regularly to the *Guardian*, the *Yorkshire Post*, the *Dalesman* and the *Barnsley Chronicle*. He has published several volumes of poetry and has been castaway on Radio 4's *Desert Island Discs*. For many years he's presented *The Verb* on Radio 3. Throughout 2010 he toured the country with The Ian McMillan Orchestra and with cartoonist Tony Husband. He's been described as 'the Shirley Bassey of performance poetry'. His latest book *Talking Myself Home* is his life story of his life told in verse. For more information visit www.ian-mcmillan.co.uk

Ian here writes in his typical haunting and playful style. His poem pays respect to the coast and the location of many happy family holidays. It is an imaginative delight.

There's an ice cream birdcall, here;

A licking of winter's wind through my hat.

I'm walking on the tops at Cleethorpes.

The wind slows me down, makes me remember

Other years, by other shores,

Other winds carrying Yorkshire thoughts

Across the Humber to Lincolnshire

And me in my hat, me in my scarf.

This is a coast that constantly redresses itself,

Where the sand always moves through the timer

Slower than a fossil or faster than a gull's swoop

Onto a spare chip curled on the salted path.

I stand and look over to Spurn Point, shifting

With history, advancing and retreating

In the cold light of Wednesday. And I'm listening

To the East Coast talking in the breeze.

A Yorkshire language, blowing down the shore

Down to chilly Lincolnshire this Winter afternoon

It's talking the language of Brid

And Whitby sentences, and a Scarborough clause

And Staithes grammar, built round fishing

And waiting for the boats, and hanging on

Through the winters that never warmed

And summers brief as a donkey ride

With the jingling, the hooves-on-sand,

The toddler holding on for dear, dear life.

The language of the meeting place

Of land and water, the shore, the littoral

In tides of memory that slip down the coast

Like clouds slip through the sky on the wind's back

Down the coast to the Humber, to Spurn

Constantly shifting and drifting sand-sculpture

That looks like itself; at least for a day, or

Half-an hour, some Spurn-time

That you can only count on your sandy fingers

In the time it takes the sand to shift again.

We've come to the caravan for the day, off season,

Like pilgrims looking for Summer.

I'm listening. I'm listening. I've just had a cuppa

and come out of the van, saying 'I'm just

going to check on Yorkshire, on Spurn, on

movement and stasis, history and geography

piled into one longbarrow of moving sand.

One sandcastle with crumbling walls.'

And they said 'Off you go , and don't be long'

But I might be. I might be as long as Spurn.

Feels to me as I listen that all my holidays

Are somehow crowding in the air that blows

Down from the Yorkshire Coast:

That tent on the tops at Whitby

That almost blew inside out in a storm

That rattled your teeth and straightened your hair;

That B&B where the woman said 'Dun't

Flush owt. Whatever you do, dun't

Flush owt.' And my dad forgot, and flushed

In the middle of the night and flushed

Red as a sunrise when she told him off

The next morning in front of the guests

And the bacon and the eggs. Outside,

A particular Scarborough rain fell, that rain

That carries in it the promise of sun.

That time when the kids were little

And we always left sandy prints

Across the hotel carpet

Like we'd come from a desert

A desert with picnics and ice cream.

There's an ice-cream birdcall, here,

Spurn Head or Spurn Point. (Yorkshire Post Newspapers)

As we go towards Spurn Head we are more and more impressed with the desolate character of the shore. The tide may be out, and only puny waves tumbling on the wet sand, and yet it is impossible to refrain from feeling that the very peacefulness of the scene is sinister, and the waters are merely digesting their last meal of boulder-clay before satisfying a fresh appetite.'
Yorkshire, Gordon Home, 1908.

A licking of Winter's wind through my hat.

I'm gazing across to Spurn and I feel Yorkshire

In the air. Somehow, I can feel my own

History blowing in the chill mist,

My Yorkshire life hanging in the air.

Maybe because my dad was a sailor

Maybe because we lived in Barnsley

About as far from the sea as you can get,

We always slipped to the coast

In the old Blue Zephyr 6, my dad driving

Like he was steering a boat, slowly, slowly,

To Thornwick Bay where we slept in a caravan

As small as a beer mat, as cramped as a pair

Of hand-me-down shoes. We walked by the sea

And I wrote a message in a glowing pop bottle

And threw it in the water and it splashed

And bobbed like a glass ship from a story

And came to rest ten yards down the beach

And a kid picked it up and opened it and read

My message, my scrawled writing that said

'My name is Ian and I live in Darfield. Will you write

To me if you find this message?' And the kid

Was as excited as this kid who chucked it in

And as excited as this big kid is now, remembering

How he ran to his dad and I turned to my dad

And the sky was a colour you'd have to call Yorkshire

The sky was a colour you'd have to call Coast.

And somehow all those memories are carried

In the wind that shapes Spurn, shapes all of us.

So I stand in the raw fridge of a Cleethorpes winter

And screw up my eyes and look at the past,

Or Spurn as I call it; it's as though all our Yorkshire stories

Have been blown to the edge of this shifting finger

Of sand. This shifting finger that erodes over the years

And builds itself back up again, differently. Time

To go back to the van. Another cup of tea, maybe a cake

And then back in the car for the drive home. I've learned

This: that the past blows back into your mind,

Like the tides, in and out and back again, shaping

The coast, shaping your life as you stand here in your hat

And remember the child you were, on all those holidays

Those Yorkshire holidays, the sand shifting under your feet

And you didn't mind a bit. Time to go back. See you, Spurn:

You'll be different next time I come. Like I will be.

Like we all will be. This ice-cream wind is making me cry.

Groynes on the beach are a feature of many coastal areas. For decades they have been built to interrupt water flow and limit the movement of sediment. The lighthouse was used until 1985 when it was decommissioned. (Yorkshire Post Newspapers)

Hull city centre - circa1950 - as it would probably have looked to the young Alan Plater. (Yorkshire Post Newspapers)

ALAN PLATER

Hull: The Surprise of a Large Town

Alan Plater CBE was one of the most prolific and talented playwrights and screenwriters of his generation. Born in Jarrow his family moved to Hull in 1938 and it was here that he grew up and found his way in the world. His successful writing career began with 18 episodes of *Z-Cars* and 30 of its sequel *Softly Softly*. Among his long list of television work are *The Biederbecke Trilogy*, *Fortunes of War*, *A Very British Coup*, *The Last of the Blonde Bombshells* and most recently *Joe Maddison's War* with a cast that included Kevin Whately, Robson Green and Derek Jacobi. In all he amassed over 300 assorted credits in radio, television, theatre and films and in the process won three BAFTAs. His name guaranteed a quality of humour, heart and humanity.

There is not enough space here to write about his enormous talent and his prodigious body of work. It was with great sadness that Alan passed away whilst working on his contribution to this book. He was writing it at the time of his death. Hull was Alan's childhood home. There is no one more qualified to write about the city. For more of the same you may look up his autobiography, *Doggin' Around*.

THESE ARE THE POETS...

1968 was a bad year in Hull. In the days when we still had a relatively buoyant fishing industry, three trawlers went down in the Arctic with the loss of fifty-nine men. This happened in the space of only ten days and left a city stunned and in mourning. The trawlers were the Ross Cleveland, the St Romanus and the Kingston Peridot.

There followed the usual passionate but ultimately inadequate responses – a promise of better safety precautions, expressions of sympathy in high places and a clutch of fund-raising events for the dependants – including a poetry-reading.

The story of the disaster is well-known and well-recorded – the poetry-reading less so, and no reason why it should be; but it has a bearing on what it is that helps make Hull unlike any other place of similar size.

I was invited to take part in the reading and – though I'm no sort of poet – agreed to turn up and read something appropriate. I arrived in good time and – accustomed as I was to readings attended by a dozen people on a good night - was taken aback to discover over thirty people in the room.

'Looks like we'll have a decent audience,' I said to one of the organisers.

'This isn't the audience. These are the poets.'

I'd never seen so many poets gathered together in one place. Not only that, when the reading began, it was

The modern port of Hull. (Yorkshire Post Newspapers)

clear they were the real thing and not versifiers or doggerel mongers.

I had written a poem for the occasion. It's called Names.

Names

Street names: Eton, Harrow, Rugby
Homage to distant headmasters
Not that they realise it.
Other names
Ross: name of a group, more powerful
than Beatles.
Cleveland, echo of distant hills,
And petrol to drive the lorries.
Ross Cleveland: name of a boat.
In the street: Eton, Harrow, or Rugby
take your pick
A lad plays football
Three goals and you're in against gable
end goalposts
Belting them past his scrub-kneed mate
Stopping to let the lorries go by
Then he's Wagstaff again
His real name's Mick

Kingston's a name: regal half of a fine city
Capital of Humberside.
Peridot: origin unknown says Oxford
meaning a kind of chrysolite,
jeweller's name for olivine.
Kingston Peridot: name of a boat.
In the football street
Eton, Harrow or Rugby
Whichever it was
Rain stops play
Slanting down between the fish-house
chimneys
That fence off the street against the sun.
Tea-time anyway.
Ta-ra Mick
See yer kid

Running up the terrace, Amethyst Terrace
  Jeweller's name again
    Origin unknown.
      Romanus is an invented name of unknown origin
        Rome: imperial majesty: Coliseum:
          public sacrifices.
            St. Romanus: name of a boat.
              Into the two-up two-down dressing
                room trots Wagstaff.
                  His real name's Mick.
                    Tea not ready.
                      Evening paper on the table.
                        Headline.
                          Transistor radio playing: and now over to
                            the newsroom
                              and tea not ready.
                                What's up Mam?
                                  Names
                                    Eton, Harrow, Rugby
                                  Take your pick
                                    What's up Mam?
                                      Names
                                        St. Romanus, Kingston-Peridot,
                                          Ross Cleveland
                                            Whichever it was
                                              Mam. What's up?

'Names' is the only proper poem I've ever written. To be sure, I've written some half-decent song lyrics and reams of mildly amusing doggerel – plus a parody of Wordsworth's Lines *Written on Westminster Bridge* that amused Philip Larkin – but nothing that I'd claim as coming within hailing distance of poetry. Of all my collected works (never mind the quality, feel the width) Names is the only piece I would never want to change, given the chance.

Two final footnotes. Eton, Harrow and Rugby were side-streets off Hessle Road, the traditional heart of the fishing community, when we had one - Sir Tom Courtenay, my oldest and best friend in the world, was from Harrow Street, and wrote about it lovingly in his memoir, Dear Tom; and Waggy was the nickname of Ken Wagstaff, a legendary Hull City striker of the 60s and 70s.

But if you read the poem to a Hull audience, none of these explanations is necessary.

The majesty of The Humber Bridge. (Yorkshire Post Newspapers)

Queen Victoria Square and Hull City Hall, circa 1950. This scene is little altered today. (Yorkshire Post Newspapers)

A schoolboy watches a paddle steamer ferry passengers across the Humber circa 1950. The service ran between Barton on Humber on the south bank and Hull (Corporation Pier) on the north bank. It was withdrawn on 24th June 1981 - the day that the Humber Bridge was opened. (Yorkshire Post Newspapers)

Before The Deep and the regeneration of the city centre began attracting thousands of visitors, Hull's public toilets were something of a tourist attraction themselves. The interior of this celebrated public convenience, on Victoria Pier, is something of a landmark in Hull. So far as 'gents' toilets go, it is rather stunning. (Rod Slater)

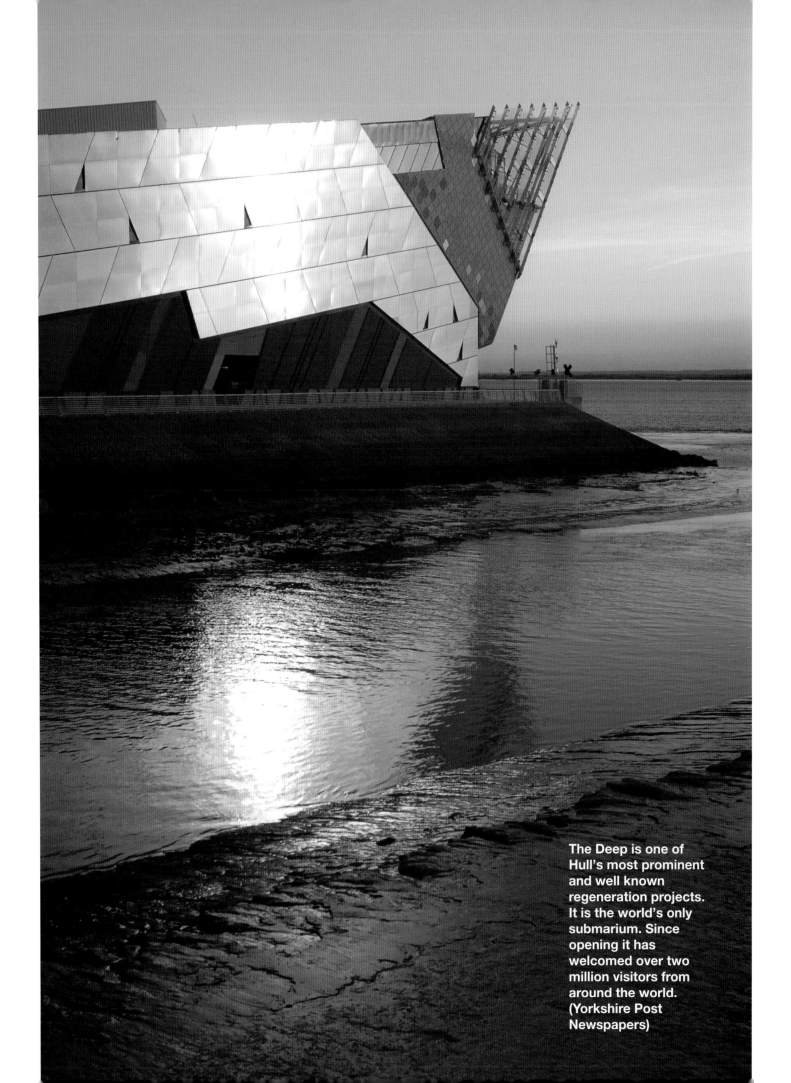

The Deep is one of Hull's most prominent and well known regeneration projects. It is the world's only submarium. Since opening it has welcomed over two million visitors from around the world. (Yorkshire Post Newspapers)

JOAN AND THE CHRISTMAS PUDDING

In between writing plays I've done a deal of teaching – on all five continents, if I'm right in thinking Israel is technically in Africa. In all these places the same two questions recur. How did you start? And what made you think you could do it?

These are perfectly legitimate and the answers both dwell in Hull and both have a poetic dimension.

In or around 1942 my class at primary school presented a Christmas play. Despite hiding under the desk (I was terrified that kissing might be involved) I ended up being cast as the Christmas pudding. My long-suffering mother made a costume designed to maximise my embarrassment, but the killer blow came with my lines.

I had to learn and recite the following stanza:

> *Ho ho I'm such a merry chap*
>
> *Without me Christmas would fall flat*
>
> *So here I am and here's my chance*
>
> *To have a jolly little dance!*

Then, hands on hips, I had to hoppity skippity around the Christmas tree, played by a little girl called Margaret. Her long-suffering mother had made the tree from a green taffeta dress on to which she had sewn such fragile glass toys that had survived the Blitz thus far. If you breathed on her another one would break and, careful as I was with my hoppities and skippeties, most of the others littered the stage in tiny glittering fragments by the end of my dance. It was the most humiliating experience of my life up to that point but what rankled the most was that verse. Even at age six I knew it was terrible. 'Chap' and 'flat' do not rhyme and never will.

I knew in my heart of hearts that I could do better and it was probably that day that a writer was born.

The early 1960s were a formative period. I'd sold a couple of radio plays (not very good) and was knocking on television's door with work that, in retrospect, I now see was mostly about what a tough job it was being a struggling young man in a place very like Hull. On the whole, television wasn't very interested.

Then I came across a quote from the great Joan Littlewood. I never traced the source, mainly because I never tried but what she said was 'You can walk the streets of Hull and hear the people speaking poetry.'

This was a big new idea. I now know that in her early days in Manchester, Joan had worked on some pioneering documentaries that included – wait for it – real ordinary working people talking!

In other words she was saying that inside everyday ordinary vernacular speech, poetry is lying in wait. As a native Tynesider, I should have known this from birth, but somehow it had never sunk in. As it happens, an example was waiting in the wings. I met a friend called Tony at the Craven Park dog-track. He worked in the building trade, which is more dangerous than people realise but even so, I was a little shocked to see his head swathed in bandages.

'What happened to you?'

'I was plastering out a bungalow we're building in Anlaby and I saw the milkman. We needed some milk for the tea so I jumped out the window to stop him.'

'So?'

'Well I forgot I was stood on a bloody plank and I banged my head on the lintel.'

'Were you knocked unconscious?'

'No, but I was rendered to my knees, sobbing.'

What gives that last line its lovely resonance is the word 'rendered' because in the plastering trade, the rendering coat was what Tony was applying when the milkman appeared.

Thus, I started to listen more carefully and Joan was right. The gold is there and it's my job to find it; and when students ask 'How do you start?' I tell them:

'Listen!'

GET STUFFED!

Some years before Screaming Lord Sutch launched his monster raving loonies on the world, a group of harmless anarchists in Hull started the Get Stuffed Party and ran several candidates at the local elections, one of whom, I recall, was Mike Waterson of the legendary folk-singing family. They won a lot of public sympathy, several column inches in the press, a few healthy laughs and hardly any votes.

But they are a good example of the subversive element that recurs in the history of the city. Perhaps it has its roots in the Civil War when, famously, Sir John Hotham turned away the King from the city gates, a gesture for which he was later executed.

In his introduction to *A Rumoured City*, a 1980 anthology of Hull-based poets, Douglas Dunn, one of a clutch of poets to find some, at least, of their voices by the tide of Humber – Philip Larkin, Roger McGough, Andrew Motion, to grab three at random – called the city 'piratical' which seems to me totally apt.

Holding hands with the subversion runs a lovely, laconic sense of the absurd.

In the window of a shoe-shop on the Holderness Road I saw a sign reading:

BUY ONE - GET ONE FREE.

On the terraces at Boothferry Park when Hull City were having one of their recurring bad spells, a man stood with a small, home-made sign bearing the single word: BOO.

But perhaps shops and shop windows are the keys to a city's soul. Maurice Lipman, father of the blessed and beloved Maureen, had a tailor's shop on Monument Bridge. It had two rooms with a connecting archway and a sign reading: READY TO WEAR DEPARTMENT - DOWNSTAIRS.

An evocative image of Hull docks taken in 1937, a year before Alan Plater's family moved from Jarrow. (Yorkshire Post Newspapers)

One day a customer plucked up the courage to ask him: 'Maurice – why do you have that sign up when there are no stairs? The place is all on the same level.'

Said Maurice: 'Well, Burtons were throwing it out and it seemed a pity to waste it.'

And a lovely guy called Norman Beedle, who worked in PR but in his spare time wrote jokes for people like Bob Monkhouse and Ken Dodd, told me he once saw a cat lying on a side of ham in a Co-op show window but, he added, 'The cat was washing itself at the time.'

But my all-time favourite example of the city's gift for subversive one-liners cropped up in a television interview when, on one of those rare occasions when we made the national news, the interviewer – a sharp suited young man with a full set of teeth – made a marginally slighting remark about Hull to his chosen spokesman for the common folks.

Came the reply: 'It's all right for you, flower. You want to try living here.'

LIVING THERE

Let me clarify the chronology of my life. I was born in Jarrow in 1935 and the family moved to Hull in 1938 when my Dad got a job in the city. I've transformed this into a cheap gag that runs: we waited until the Depression was over then headed to Hull to be in good time for the Blitz.

Aside from four years at university in my beloved Newcastle, I then lived in Hull until 1984, when I moved to London with my second wife, Shirley Rubinstein.

According to my arithmetic, that means I lived in Hull for approximately 42 years, which has to be a fair basis on which to be opinionated and dogmatic.

A couple of odd things happened in London. I settled into the city in about twenty minutes but paradoxically became much more of a professional Northerner.

Here's an example. We were at a dinner party comprising four or five couples, all of them left-wing media folk. Their main preoccupation seemed to be the cost of school fees - they certainly went on about it at great length, and loudly. Eventually I cracked and held my hand up like a primary school kid who needs to go to the lavatory. The table fell silent and I said:

'Shirley and I have six kids between us, all state-educated in Hull and the East Riding but somehow they've ended up with six university degrees, including two Firsts and a Ph.D. And it didn't cost us a penny. Where did we go wrong?'

The effect was a startled silence, as if I'd farted in the salmon mousse. Then the odd mumbled response along the lines of: 'Well of course, you were so lucky, living in the North,' – this from a group of people who mainly knew the North as the region you fly over on the way to the Edinburgh Festival.

At another dinner party a few weeks later I complained that the main difficulty about moving to London was the servant problem – and was taken totally seriously.

All this is good knockabout stuff but it does illustrate aspects of the cultural divide that exists in our green and pleasant land. When Shirley moved to Hull in her earlier life, she had the drains cleaned, before a friendly neighbour explained that the smell was coming from the fish dock – though, on a pedantic note – the smell was from the fish meal factory, where people processed those parts of the fish considered unfit for human consumption. Today the fishing industry has gone and the city smells much better.

Shirley was also touched by the way total strangers addressed her as 'petal' or 'flower' – none of which has ever made Hull an earthly paradise.

A NORTH-EAST COAST TOWN

One of the many paradoxes surrounding the city is that despite my obvious affection for the place, it isn't a view shared by the world at large. Every so often, media folk with nothing better to do mastermind a survey or opinion poll asking the question: what is the lousiest place to live in the UK and Hull generally comes in the first three. Sometimes we win.

I have no idea how many people are consulted, who they are and frankly I don't give a damn: but I will concede a couple of flaws in the demi-paradise.

The first is half-way between an inferiority complex and a chip on the shoulder.

This, I believe, has its roots in the Second World War when Hull, proportionately, was the most bombed city in the land – right up there with Coventry and London but crucially nobody knew about it, apart from the citizens, obviously.

On the BBC news we were always identified as 'a North-East coast town'. This was apparently for security reasons, which implies that the Germans didn't know where they were dropping bombs. We thought it was very odd and a bit unfair.

There was a parallel situation during the great floods of 2007 when the network news concentrated on the West Riding, with the nation's ace intrepid reporters striding around in thigh boots. Our floods were less dramatic visually, but the long-term effects are with the city to this day. Hull only made the network news when the Council hired a PR firm to kick in a few doors of the relevant newsrooms.

In these circumstances, a small chip on the shoulder is totally understandable.

The other flaw – and here we have nobody to blame but ourselves – is that the city can be a little slow on the uptake – like 39 years. In my case it all began with a dry stone wall in Derbyshire.

I started writing for the theatre in the 1960's and make no mistake – for many of us it was, and remains, a golden age. My early plays were produced at the Victoria Theatre, Stoke-on-Trent, by the brave and occasionally reckless Peter Cheeseman – reckless in the sense that nobody else in the Potteries seemed very interested in my work. My first ever opening night had an audience of four paying customers plus a clutch of local critics and friends though in fairness to everybody concerned, there was a blizzard raging outside and you could see the dialogue emerging from the actors' mouths in vapour form.

Driving home from Stoke on a wet Sunday, the car skidded off the road and collided with a stationary dry stone wall. *Two-Way Family Favourites* was on the radio and Dusty Springfield was singing: 'In the Middle of

Imported cars await collection. The port of Hull still handles around 13 million tonnes of cargo each year and employs several thousand people. (Yorkshire Post Newspapers)

Twilight on the Humber. (Yorkshire Post Newspapers)

Nowhere'. The thought that came into my mind was: if we had a producing theatre in Hull, life would be much more secure. There are no dry stone walls lining the roads anywhere in the city.

We formed a committee of like-minded citizens and set to work. The aim was very simple: to build a purpose-made Theatre and Arts Centre, 'a workshop and a shop window' to quote our fund-raising appeal. Local authority support was crucial and, oddly enough, fashionable and we could cite the Nottingham Playhouse, the Coventry Belgrade and the Sheffield Crucible in evidence. In retrospect, the sums of money seem ludicrous. We asked for £5,000 towards the building costs and another £5,000 towards running costs. The City Council, which had gone briefly Tory gave us £250 'as a gesture of goodwill'.

We didn't get our palace of culture. Courtesy of a friendly vicar we got an old and unwanted church hall in Spring Street, not at the time the most salubrious street in the city but, as one of our supporters pointed out, it was very handy for the morgue and the abattoir.

One of my last acts on leaving the city in 1984 was to be on a selection panel that appointed John Godber as the new artistic director of Hull Truck. Twenty-five years later he's still running the store, having created a large and loyal audience, many of them what we no longer apparently call working class: let's settle for common folk. Many theatres have set out with this ambition but few have succeeded. Not only that but thanks to John's talent, hard work and the sheer bloody-mindedness of his team, the theatre now has a shiny state-of-the-art building in the heart of the city centre and well away from the morgue. It cost £17,000,000 with a handsome contribution and undeviating support from the Lib-Dem council. Whichever way you do the sums, it's a giant step from £250 as a gesture of goodwill. You might also argue that 39 years is a long time for an idea to sink in: but democracy often takes time.

SOMETIMES WE'RE AHEAD OF THE FIELD

Early in the twentieth century a strange-looking device appeared on the scene. It was called a telephone. The government of the day examined it and came to the sensible conclusion: public utility–public ownership. However, some sharp guy in Hull spotted Clause 337B (this is guesswork) which gave local authorities the chance to opt out. Thus was born what became known as the Hull Corporation Telephones Department. It was a triumph and an elegant joke that places like Manchester and Birmingham apparently concluded that these new-fangled devices would never catch on. As the great man once said: so it goes.

The results on the ground were dramatic. Despite paying a handsome annual sum in hard cash to the GPO for the use of their facilities, our phone bills were consistently 30% less than those of lesser mortals outside of the city. It was something else to boast about over North London dinner tables

But there is a striking contrast if you're on the lookout for such. On the one hand, a local authority that needs 39 years to make up its mind; on the other, a parallel administration that sees the potential in telecommunications 100 years before the word has entered the national vocabulary.

Of course, there were unpredictable wobbles along, notably caused by the long shadows of a grocer's daughter from Grantham, who believed public ownership was a deadly sin much worse than coveting your neighbour's ox, ass or servant. Sell, sell, sell, came the clarion call from Downing Street. The market knows best — a slogan that gives off a hollow ring in A.D. 2010.

The response managed to please some of the people some of the time, which isn't bad for a democracy. The council sold 49% of the company, with the citizenry – AKA the common folk – getting first whack at knock-down prices. One family I know – husband, wife and three kids, who'd never seen a stock or a share in their lives – made enough of an overnight killing to finance a rare, and possibly unique, continental holiday.

At the other extreme, the council found itself perched on a huge pile of cash which it used, among other things, to pay for the KC Stadium – a new home for Hull City Football Club andHull Rugby League Club – as well as an impressive range of educational and recreational facilities. Public ownership again – you know it makes sense!

Other beneficiaries were millennium projects including The Deep, a massive aquarium which also acts as a deeply serious homage to the fish that gave Hull its spasmodic spurts of prosperity. It's also a beautiful and spectacular waterfront building, designed by Sir Terence Farrell.

And I'm pretty sure Hull Truck scored for a few bob too.

Whitby Beach Scene – George Weatherill (1810-1890)
(courtesy of Walker Galleries of Harrogate)

Runswick – Albert George Stevens (1863 - 1925)
(Image from the Simon Wood Collection of Staithes Group Paintings
at Brockfield Hall, York - www.brockfieldhall.co.uk)

Robin Hood's Bay – Hubert Thornley (1858 - 1898)
(private collection)

Staithes – Henry Barlow Carter (1804 - 1868)
(courtesy of TB & R Jordon)

Index of Place Names